FULL TILT BOOGIE™

BOOK 1

ALEX DE CAMPI   EDUARDO OCAÑA

INTRODUCTION

I GREW UP IN A DARK AND MISERABLE AGE WITH VERY LITTLE ANIME. BUT, IF YOU TIMED GETTING HOME FROM SCHOOL JUST RIGHT, OR YOU SEIZED CONTROL OF THE TELLY EARLY enough on a Saturday, you could watch badly-dubbed versions of **Gatchaman** (English Title: **Battle of the Planets**) and **Space Battleship Yamato** (English Title: **Star Blazers**). I ate them up. They were my **Star Wars**: cool super sentai teams with girls that got to do stuff and had good outfits, and the brave soldiers of the Yamato fighting their way through space to Iscandar in their jury-rigged ship.

Full Tilt Boogie was begun as my love song to these great space anime sagas I'd grown up with: a huge universe rich in history and mystery that we let unfold gradually through the eyes of teenage bounty hunter Tee and her family, and through the externally created family of the young Luxine Knights sent to destroy her for picking up the wrong stray. No good deed goes unpunished, as they say.

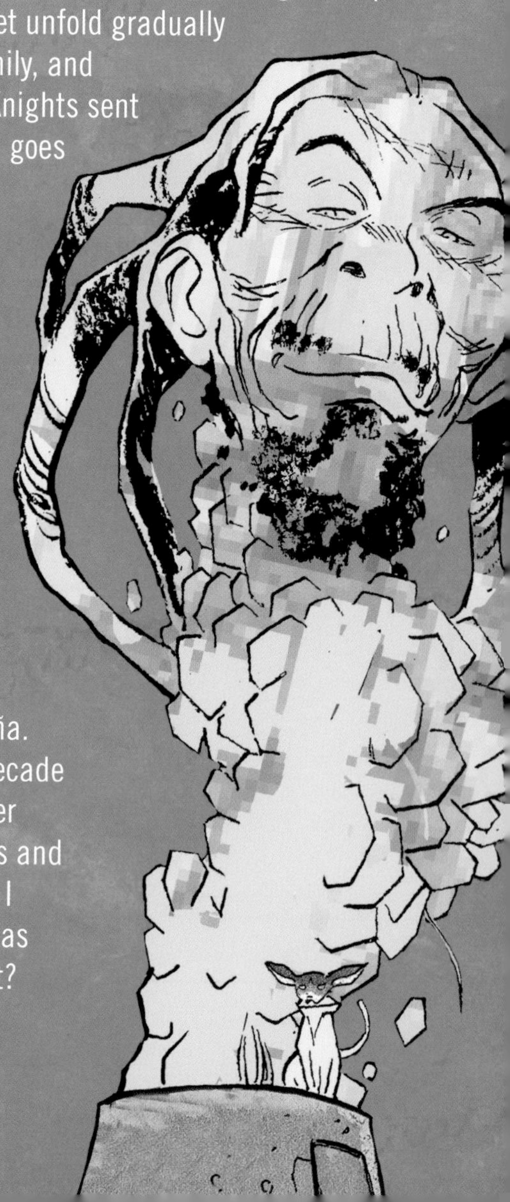

At the time I wrote *Full Tilt Boogie*, I was taking care of my own mother (I still am), and I'm a single mum to my daughter. The idea of non-symmetrical but loving and supportive families — or families that have been consciously whittled down to only their loving and supportive members — was very much on my mind. Tee and Grandma and Cat in their old ship, flying around, trying to make a buck in an intergalactic gig economy where the distances have gotten bigger but the pay hasn't gotten any better, there's some real life tucked in there.

This book wouldn't be the visual feast it is without Ed Ocaña. He and I worked together on a BD for Humanoïdes over a decade ago, and we stayed friends. We always wanted to do another project together. He's so good at creating unique characters and complex but real environments, so when Tharg asked me if I had any zarjaz tales for younger readers lying around, Ed was the first person I called with my ideas. What happened next? Well, turn the page and find out.

— ALEX DE CAMPI

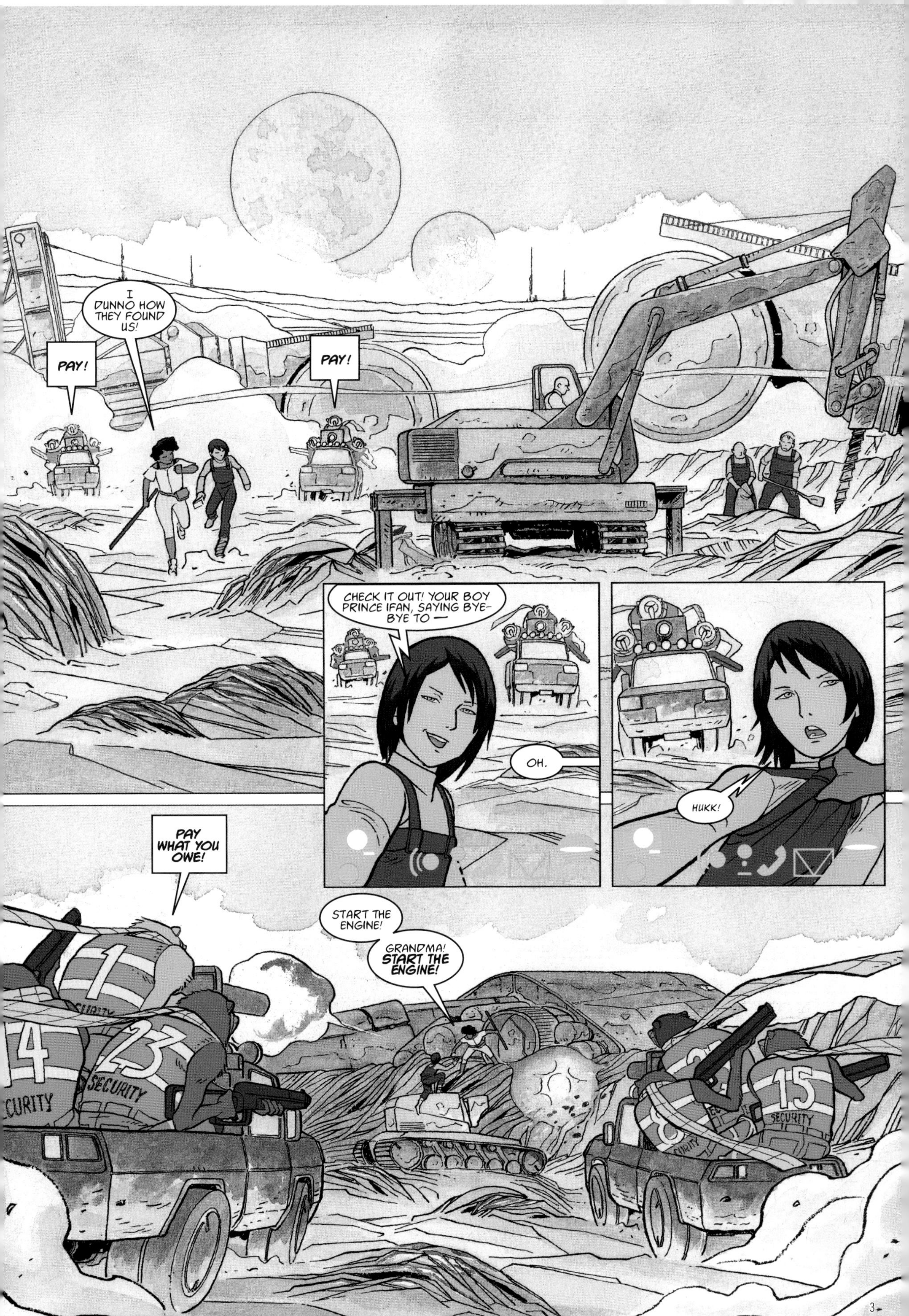

I DUNNO HOW THEY FOUND US!
PAY!
PAY!
CHECK IT OUT! YOUR BOY PRINCE IFAN, SAYING BYE-BYE TO —
OH.
HUKK!
PAY WHAT YOU OWE!
START THE ENGINE!
GRANDMA! START THE ENGINE!
1
SECURITY
4
23
SECURITY
SECURITY
15
SECURITY

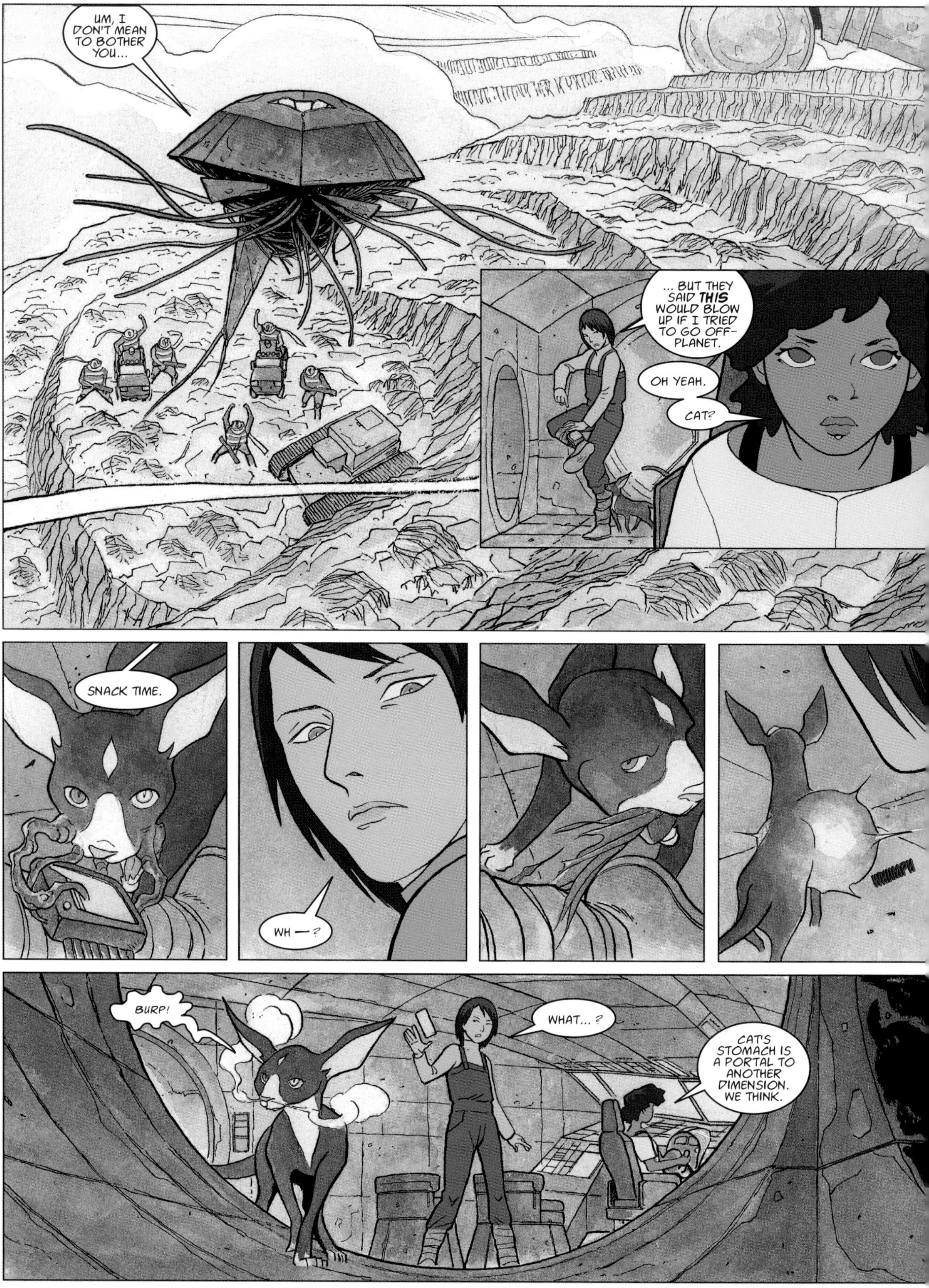
UM, I DON'T MEAN TO BOTHER YOU...
... BUT THEY SAID THIS WOULD BLOW UP IF I TRIED TO GO OFF-PLANET.
OH YEAH.
CAT?
SNACK TIME.
WH —?
WHUMPH
BURP!
WHAT...?
CAT'S STOMACH IS A PORTAL TO ANOTHER DIMENSION. WE THINK.

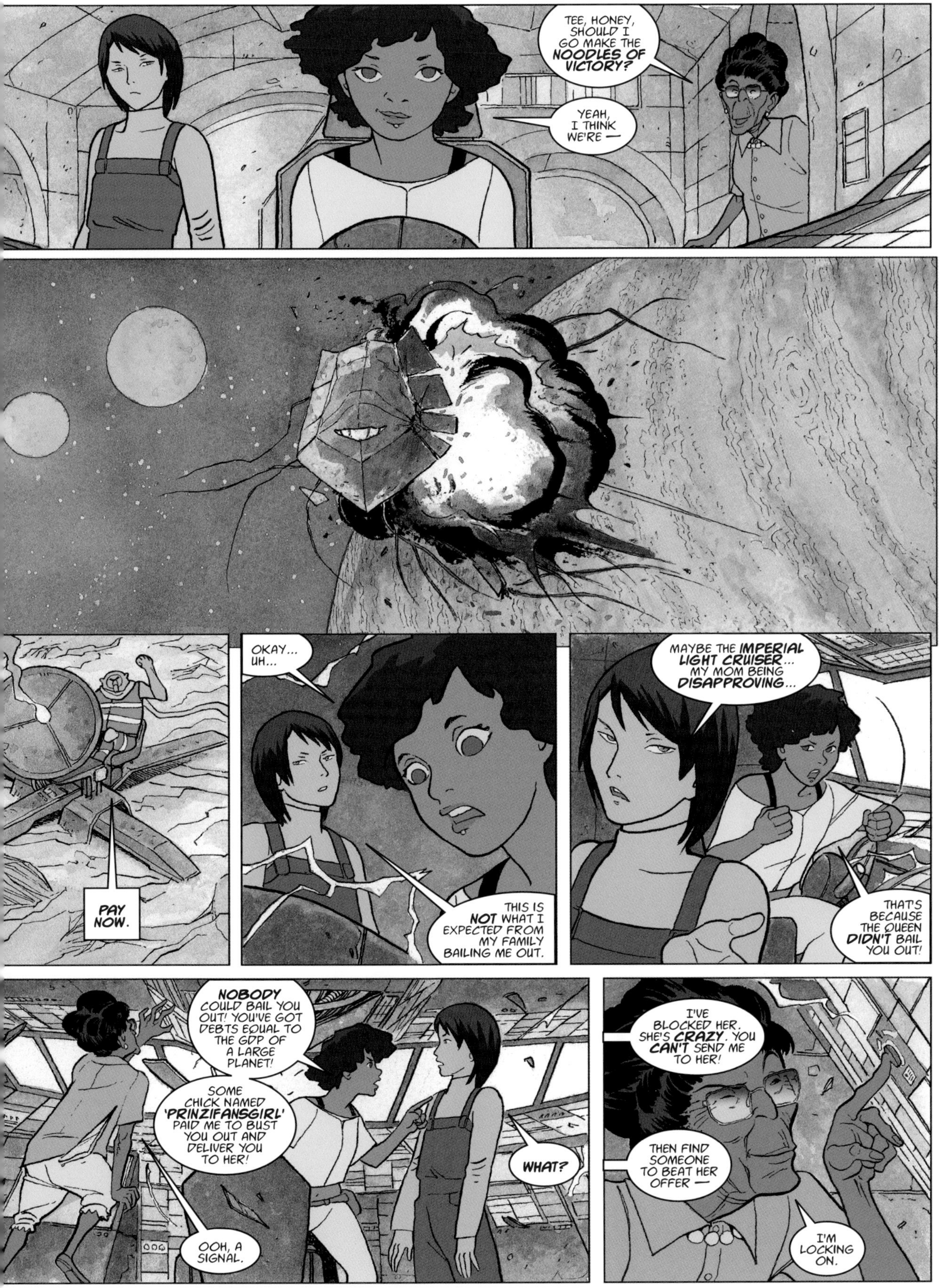

TEE, HONEY, SHOULD I GO MAKE THE **NOODLES OF VICTORY?**
YEAH, I THINK WE'RE —
PAY NOW.
OKAY... UH...
THIS IS **NOT** WHAT I EXPECTED FROM MY FAMILY BAILING ME OUT.
MAYBE THE **IMPERIAL LIGHT CRUISER**... MY MOM BEING **DISAPPROVING**...
THAT'S BECAUSE THE QUEEN **DIDN'T** BAIL YOU OUT!
NOBODY COULD BAIL YOU OUT! YOU'VE GOT DEBTS EQUAL TO THE GDP OF A LARGE PLANET!
SOME CHICK NAMED **'PRINZIFANSGIRL'** PAID ME TO BUST YOU OUT AND DELIVER YOU TO HER!
WHAT?
OOH, A SIGNAL.
I'VE BLOCKED HER. SHE'S **CRAZY**. YOU **CAN'T** SEND ME TO HER!
THEN FIND SOMEONE TO BEAT HER OFFER —
I'M LOCKING ON.

THAT'S WHY THE **BORROWER BEARS** CHOSE IT FOR THEIR DEBTORS' PRISON. NO NEIGHBOURS.

THAT'S AN OLD **LUXINE WAR** MILITARY FREQUENCY...

HUH. THERE **SHOULDN'T** BE A SIGNAL OUT HERE. THIS SECTOR'S BEEN ABANDONED FOR **CENTURIES**.

... WHAT? I AM A **PRINCE** OF LUXOS. I KNOW MY EMPIRE'S HISTORY!

YOUR BIO SAID YOU STUDIED **ART** HISTORY.

I'M JU SAYING TH SOME REAL BAD STUFF W DONE IN THAT W AND MAYBE SHOULDN'T MES

DEFINITELY DIE IN OUTER SPACE...

... OR **MAYBE** DIE FROM SOMETHING THAT HASN'T CAUSED ANY HARM FOR TWO THOUSAND YEARS.

AAH!

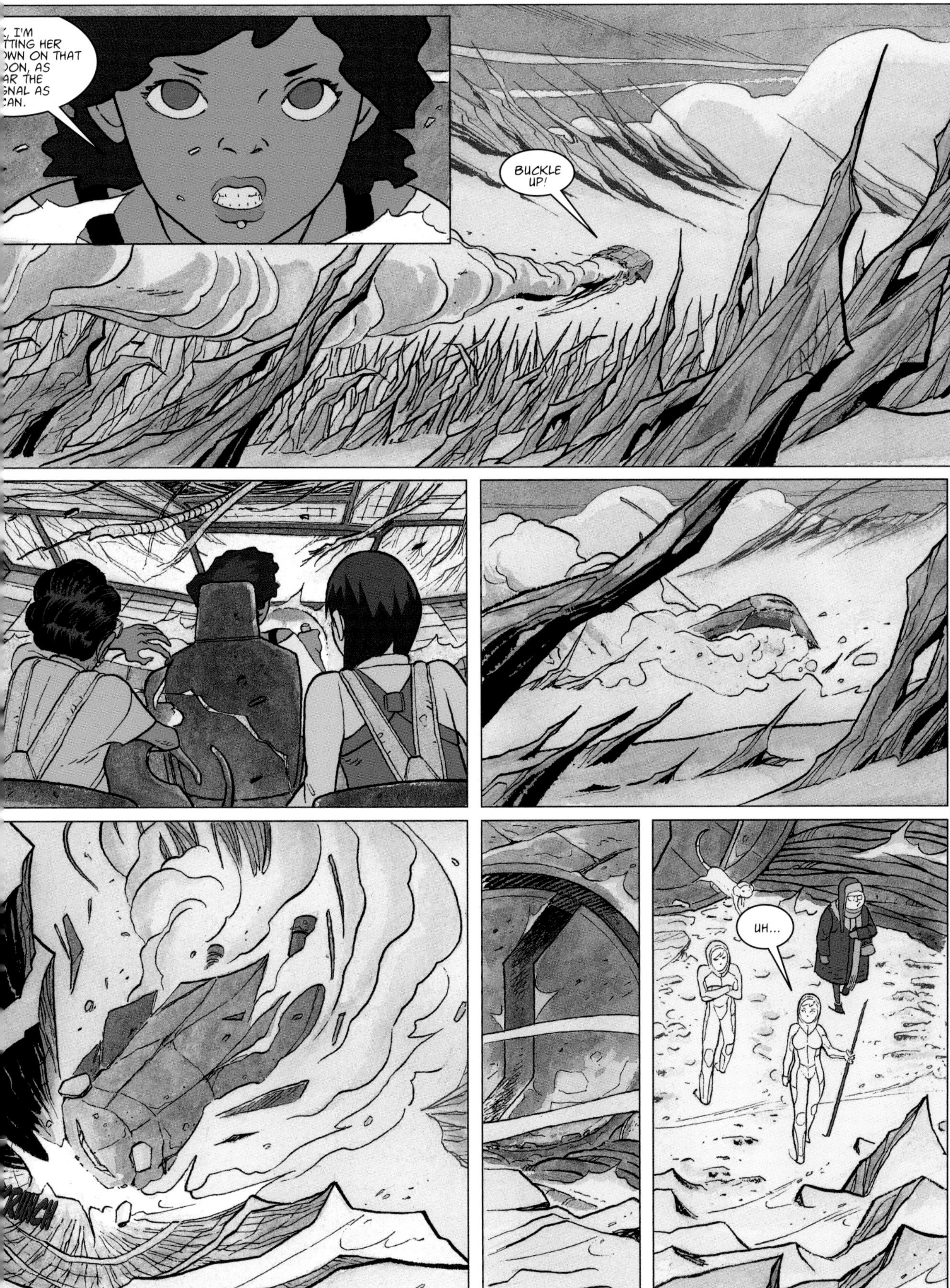
, I'M
TTING HER
WN ON THAT
OON, AS
AR THE
GNAL AS
CAN.
BUCKLE UP!
UH...

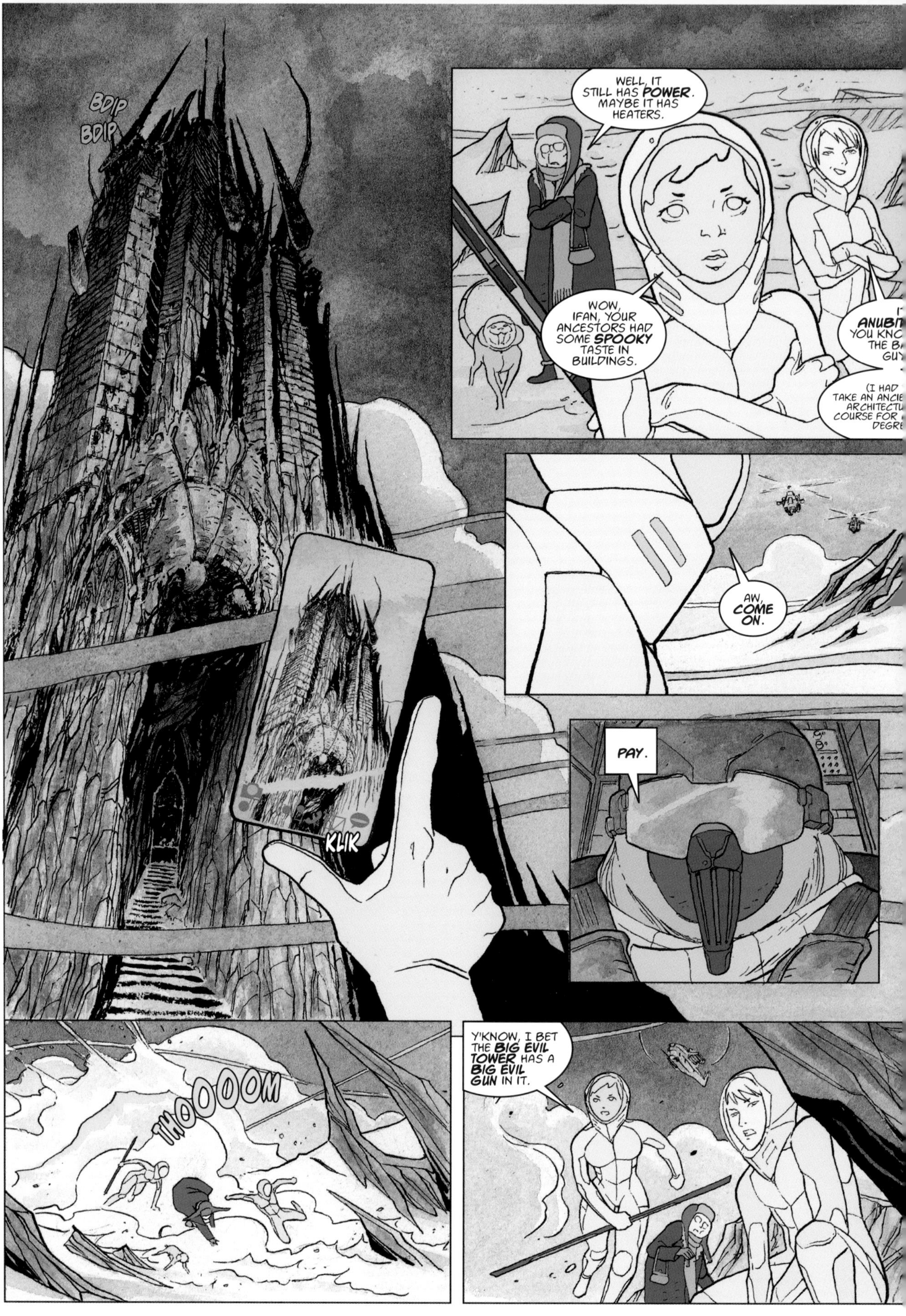
BDIP
BDIP
WELL, IT STILL HAS POWER. MAYBE IT HAS HEATERS.
WOW, IFAN, YOUR ANCESTORS HAD SOME SPOOKY TASTE IN BUILDINGS.
KLIK
AW, COME ON.
PAY.
THOOOOOM
Y'KNOW, I BET THE BIG EVIL TOWER HAS A BIG EVIL GUN IN IT.

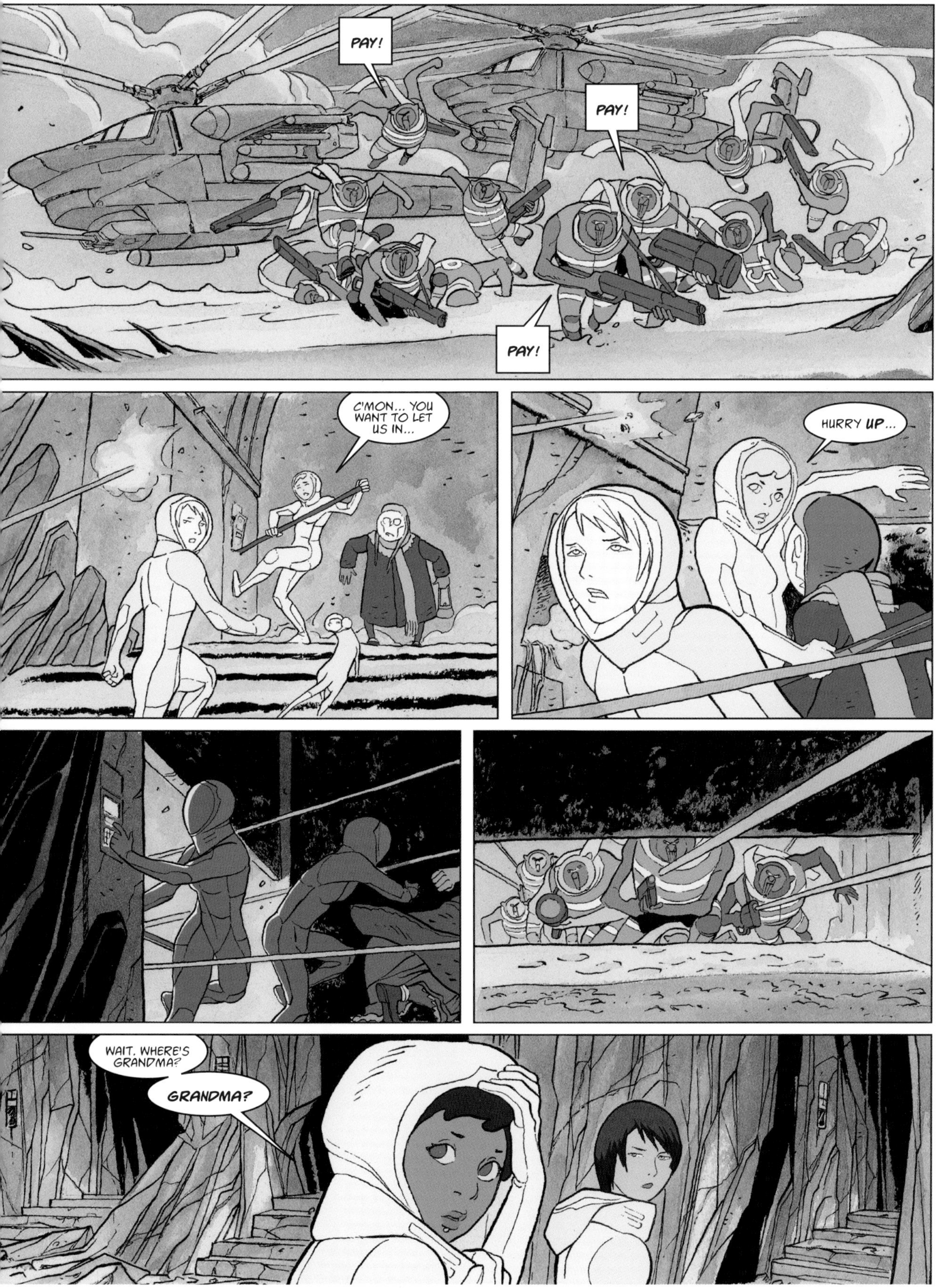
PAY!
PAY!
PAY!
C'MON... YOU WANT TO LET US IN...
HURRY UP...
WAIT. WHERE'S GRANDMA?
GRANDMA?

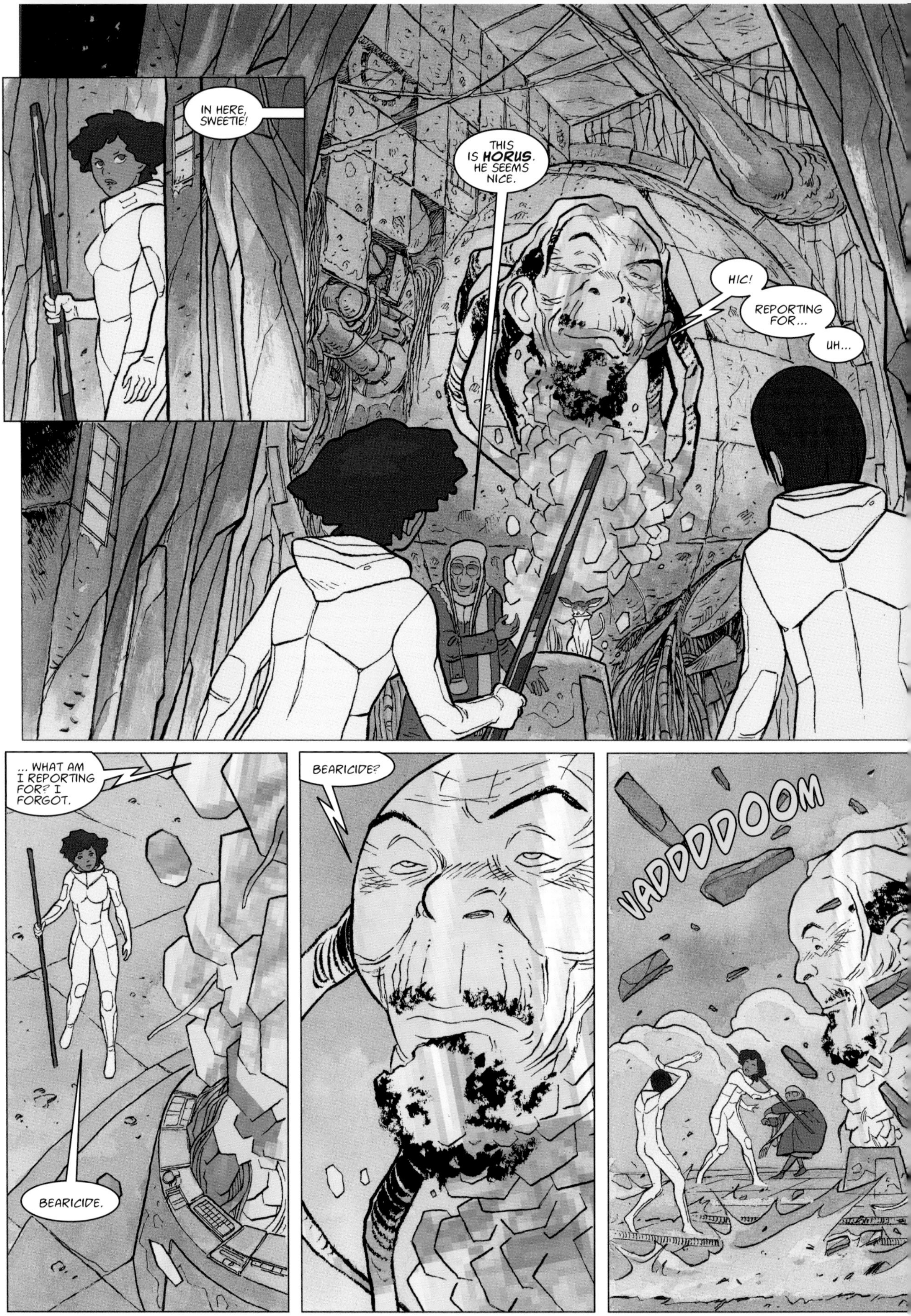

IN HERE, SWEETIE!
THIS IS HORUS. HE SEEMS NICE.
HIC!
REPORTING FOR...
UH...
... WHAT AM I REPORTING FOR? I FORGOT.
BEARICIDE.
BEARICIDE?
VADDDDOOM

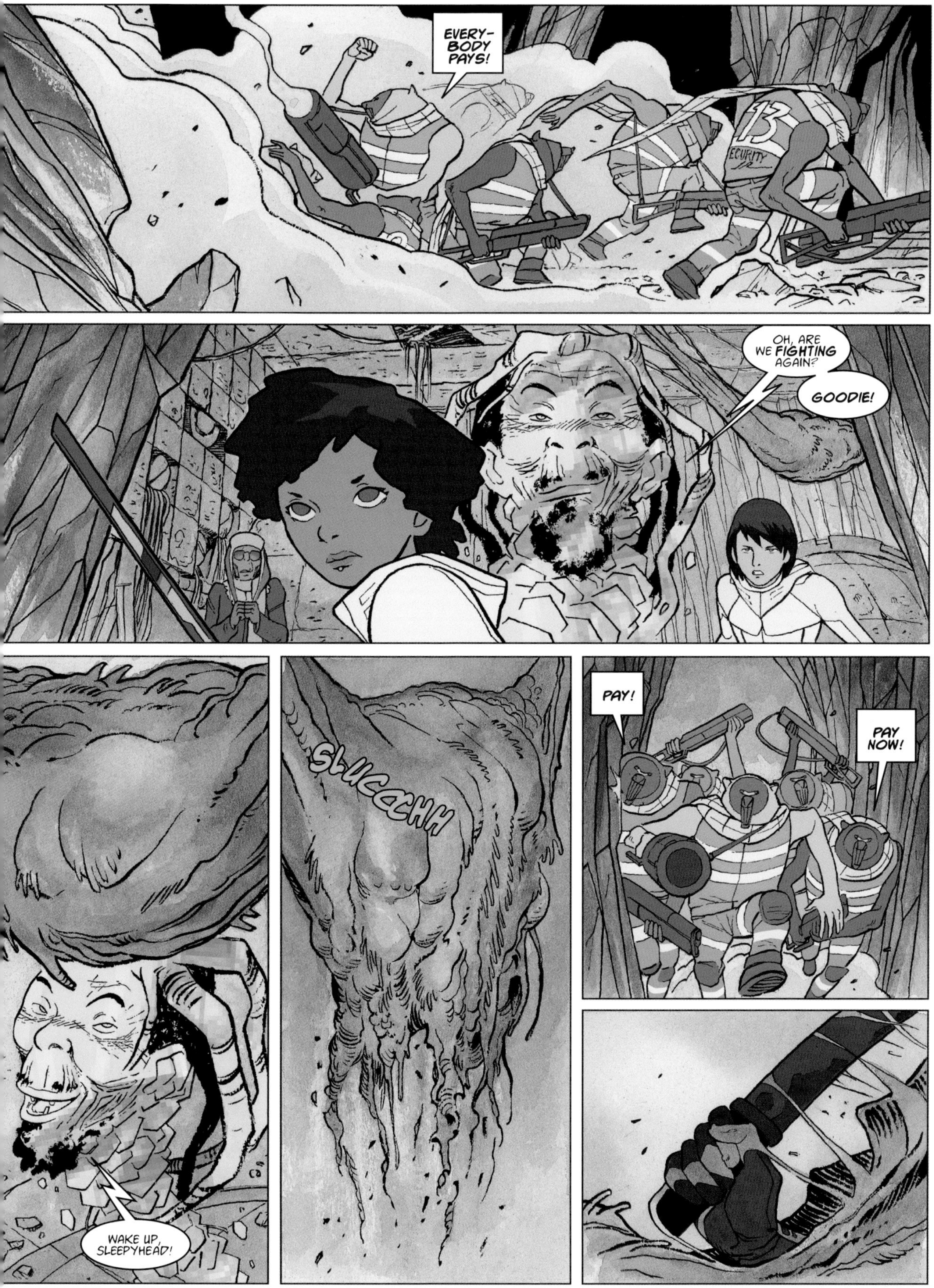
EVERY-BODY PAYS!
OH, ARE WE FIGHTING AGAIN?
GOODIE!
WAKE UP, SLEEPYHEAD!
SHUCCHH
PAY!
PAY NOW!

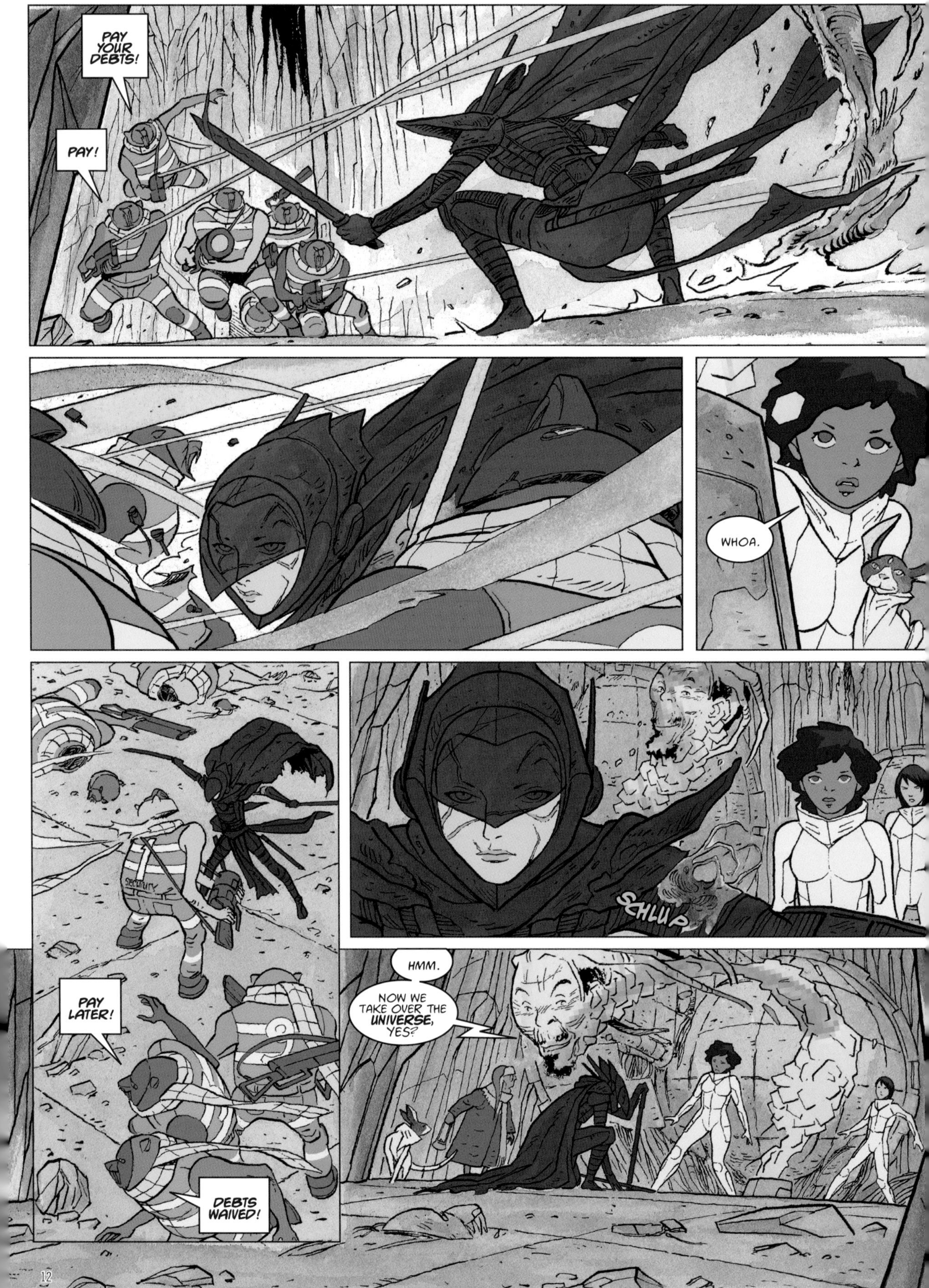
PAY YOUR DEBTS!
PAY!
WHOA.
SCHLUP
PAY LATER!
DEBTS WAIVED!
HMM.
NOW WE TAKE OVER THE UNIVERSE, YES?

A UNIVERSE AT WAR.

THE FINAL CONFRONTATION.

THE ANUBITE HORDE: RECYCLED SOULS FROM FALLEN SOLDIERS OF BOTH SIDES TO DIE AND DIE AGAIN IN BODIES GROWN OF UNHOLY SCIENCE.

AN EMPIRE FEEDING OFF WAR ITSELF.

THE LUXINE KNIGHTS: A BRAVERY VERGING ON THE FANATIC.

ROGUE ELEMENT.

PROCEED?

AN ULTIMATE SANCTION.

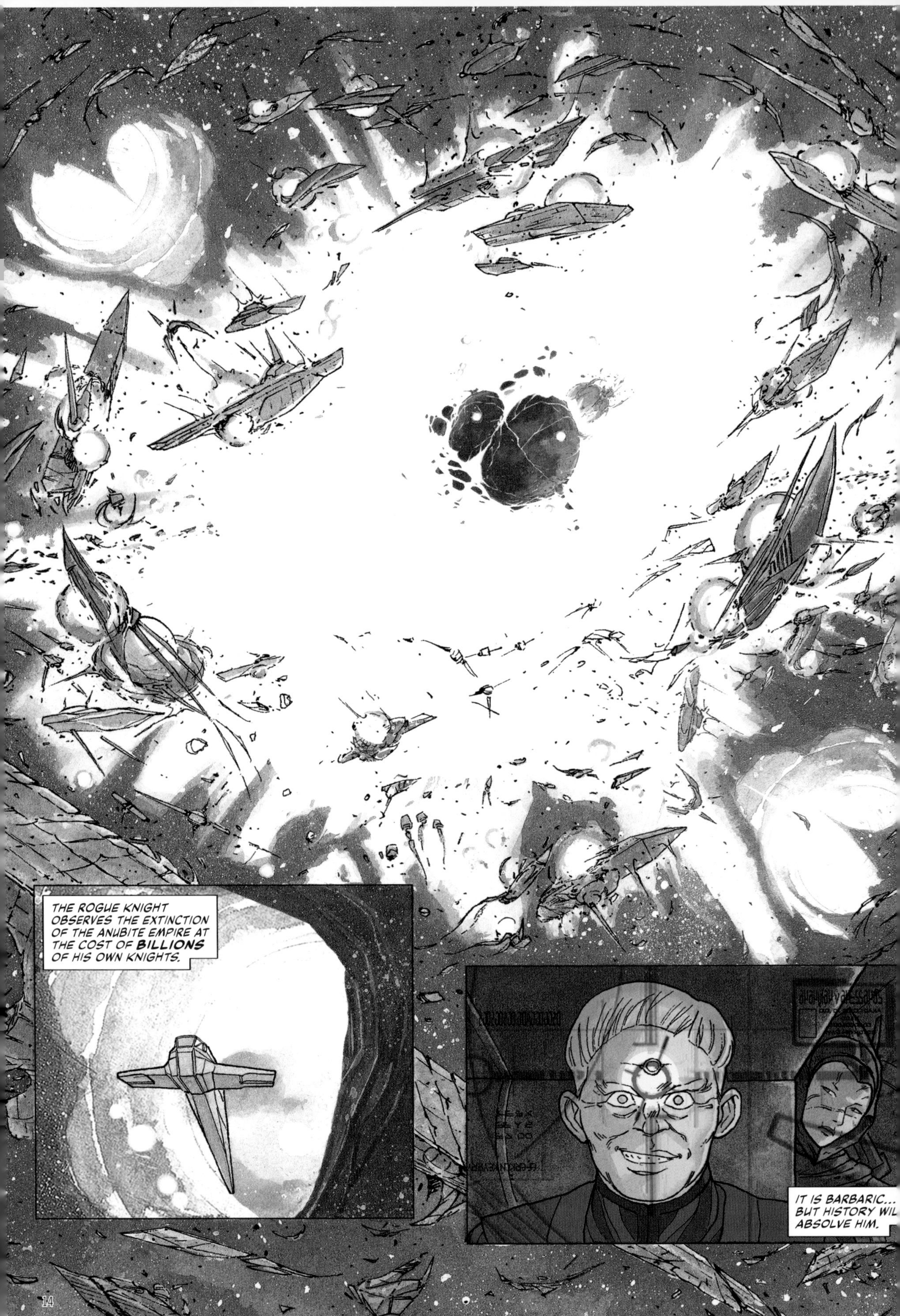
THE ROGUE KNIGHT OBSERVES THE EXTINCTION OF THE ANUBITE EMPIRE AT THE COST OF BILLIONS OF HIS OWN KNIGHTS.
IT IS BARBARIC... BUT HISTORY WIL ABSOLVE HIM.

HISTORY IS ALWAYS KIND TO THE WINNER.

THE BLACK DOG FLINCHES.

THE COMMAND VOICE HAD... STOPPED.

BUT THE SOUL-KNIFE HAD ALREADY BEGUN ITS DESCENT--

THE BLACK DOG FINISHED THE CUT.

WAR, AFTER ALL, IS MAINLY A THING OF MOMENTUM.

THE BLACK DOG WAITED FOR FURTHER INSTRUCTIONS...

...BUT THERE WOULD BE NONE.

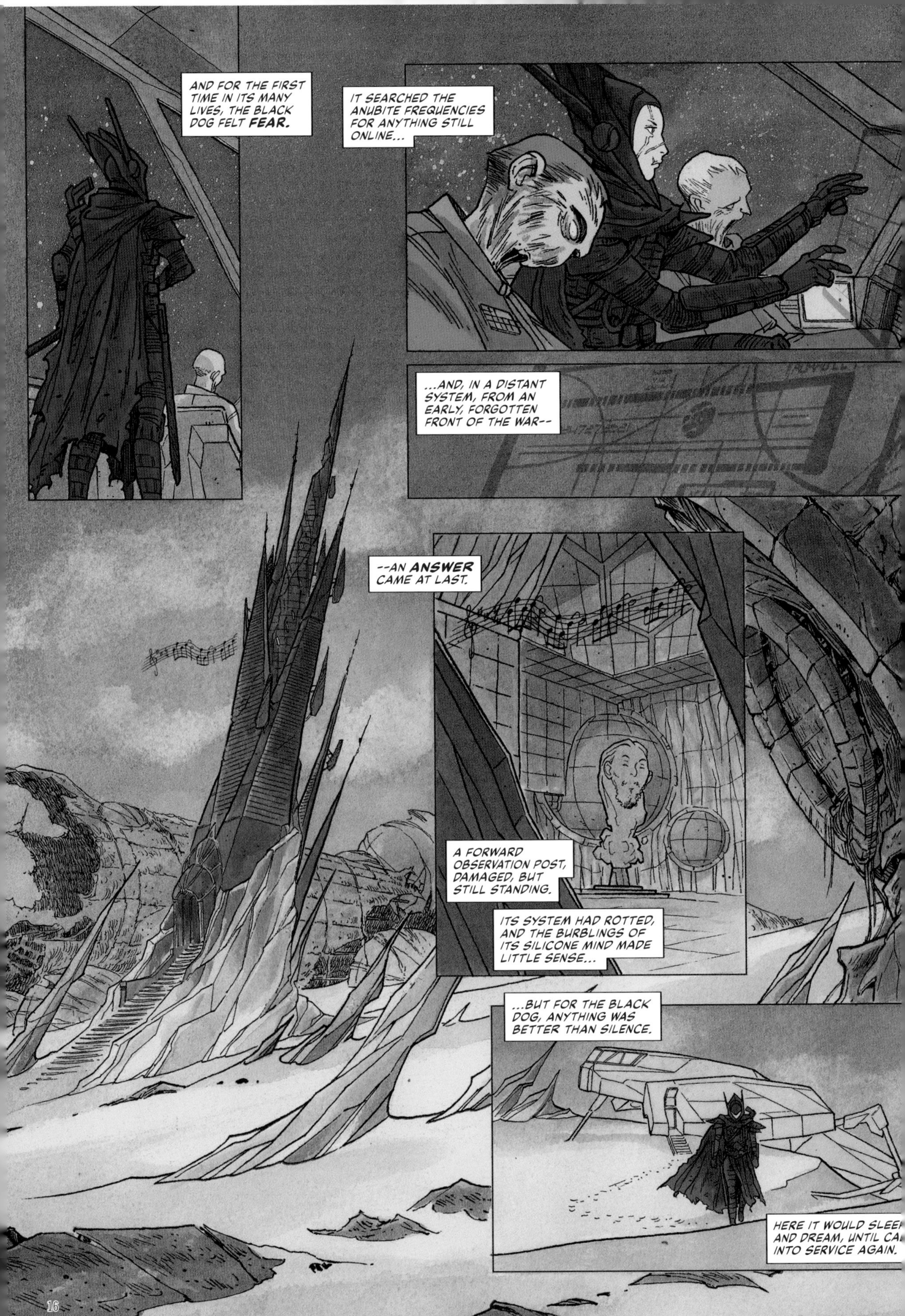

AND FOR THE FIRST TIME IN ITS MANY LIVES, THE BLACK DOG FELT **FEAR.**
IT SEARCHED THE ANUBITE FREQUENCIES FOR ANYTHING STILL ONLINE...
...AND, IN A DISTANT SYSTEM, FROM AN EARLY, FORGOTTEN FRONT OF THE WAR--
--AN **ANSWER** CAME AT LAST.
A FORWARD OBSERVATION POST, DAMAGED, BUT STILL STANDING.
ITS SYSTEM HAD ROTTED, AND THE BURBLINGS OF ITS SILICONE MIND MADE LITTLE SENSE...
...BUT FOR THE BLACK DOG, ANYTHING WAS BETTER THAN SILENCE.
HERE IT WOULD SLEE
AND DREAM, UNTIL CA
INTO SERVICE AGAIN.

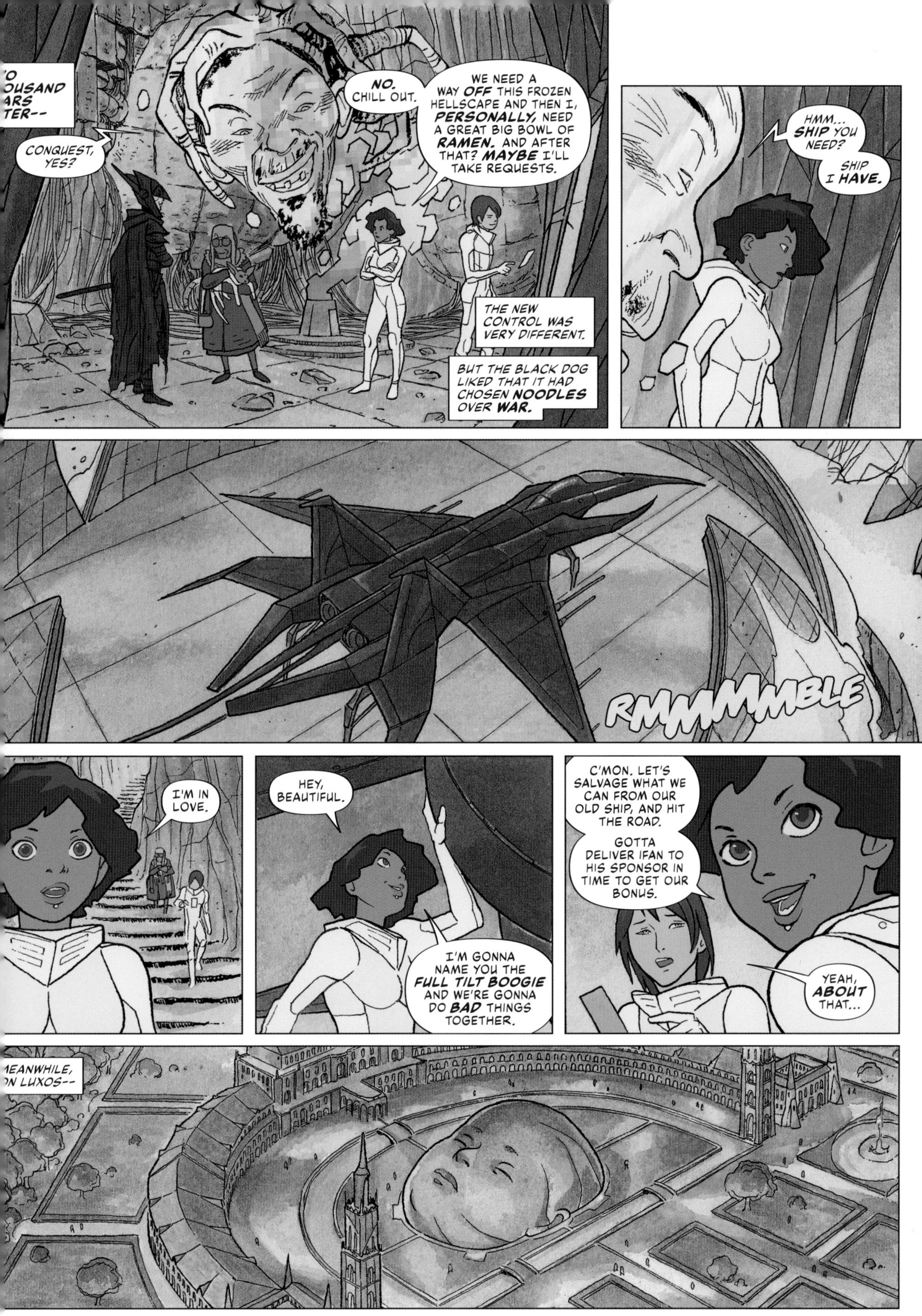

TO
OUSAND
ARS
TER--
CONQUEST, YES?
NO. CHILL OUT.
WE NEED A WAY OFF THIS FROZEN HELLSCAPE AND THEN I, PERSONALLY, NEED A GREAT BIG BOWL OF RAMEN. AND AFTER THAT? MAYBE I'LL TAKE REQUESTS.
THE NEW CONTROL WAS VERY DIFFERENT.
BUT THE BLACK DOG LIKED THAT IT HAD CHOSEN NOODLES OVER WAR.
HMM... SHIP YOU NEED?
SHIP I HAVE.
RMMMMBLE
I'M IN LOVE.
HEY, BEAUTIFUL.
I'M GONNA NAME YOU THE FULL TILT BOOGIE AND WE'RE GONNA DO BAD THINGS TOGETHER.
C'MON. LET'S SALVAGE WHAT WE CAN FROM OUR OLD SHIP, AND HIT THE ROAD.
GOTTA DELIVER IFAN TO HIS SPONSOR IN TIME TO GET OUR BONUS.
YEAH, ABOUT THAT...
MEANWHILE,
ON LUXOS--

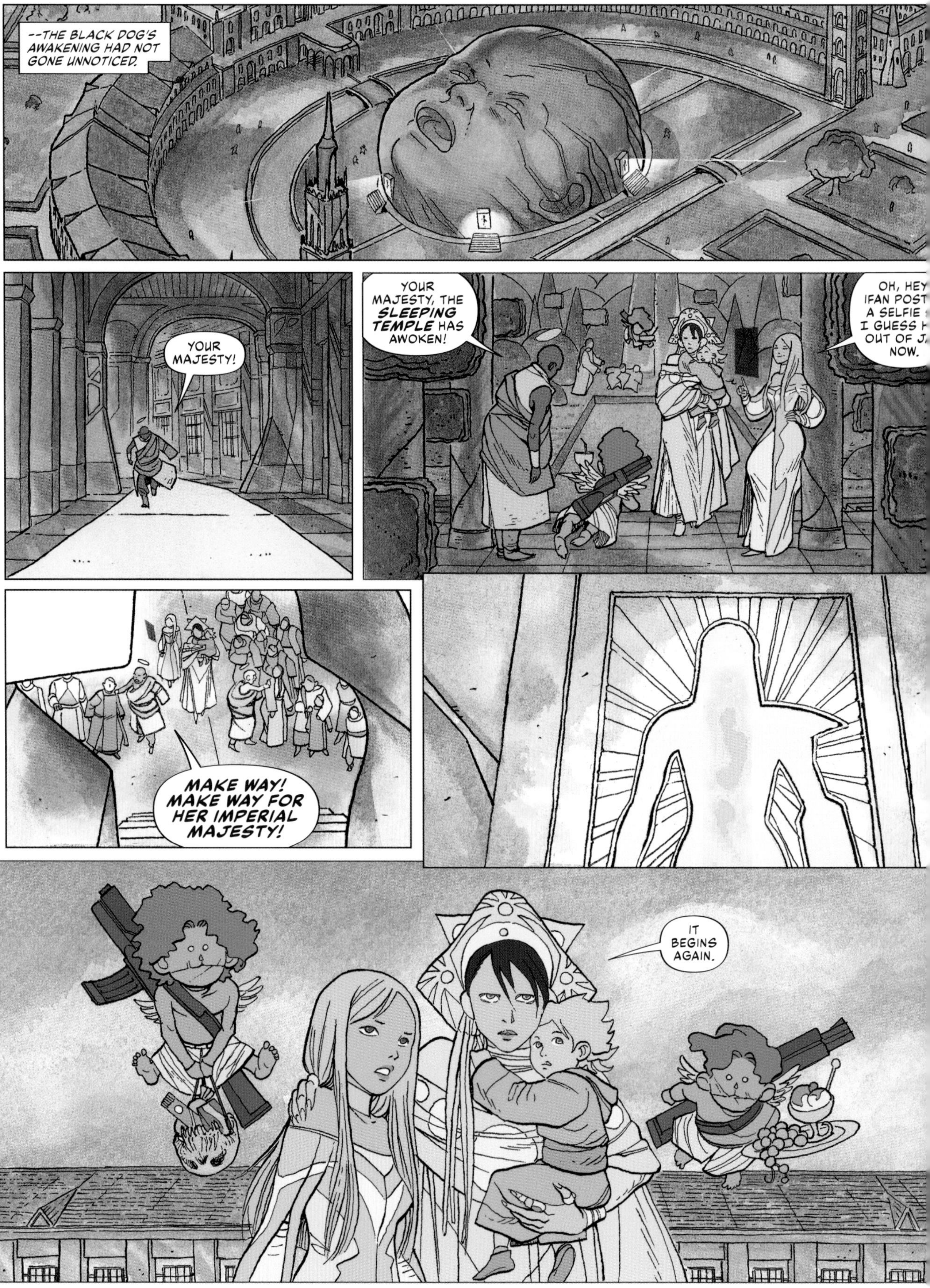
--THE BLACK DOG'S AWAKENING HAD NOT GONE UNNOTICED.
YOUR MAJESTY!
YOUR MAJESTY, THE SLEEPING TEMPLE HAS AWOKEN!
OH, HEY IFAN POST A SELFIE I GUESS H OUT OF J NOW.
MAKE WAY! MAKE WAY FOR HER IMPERIAL MAJESTY!
IT BEGINS AGAIN.

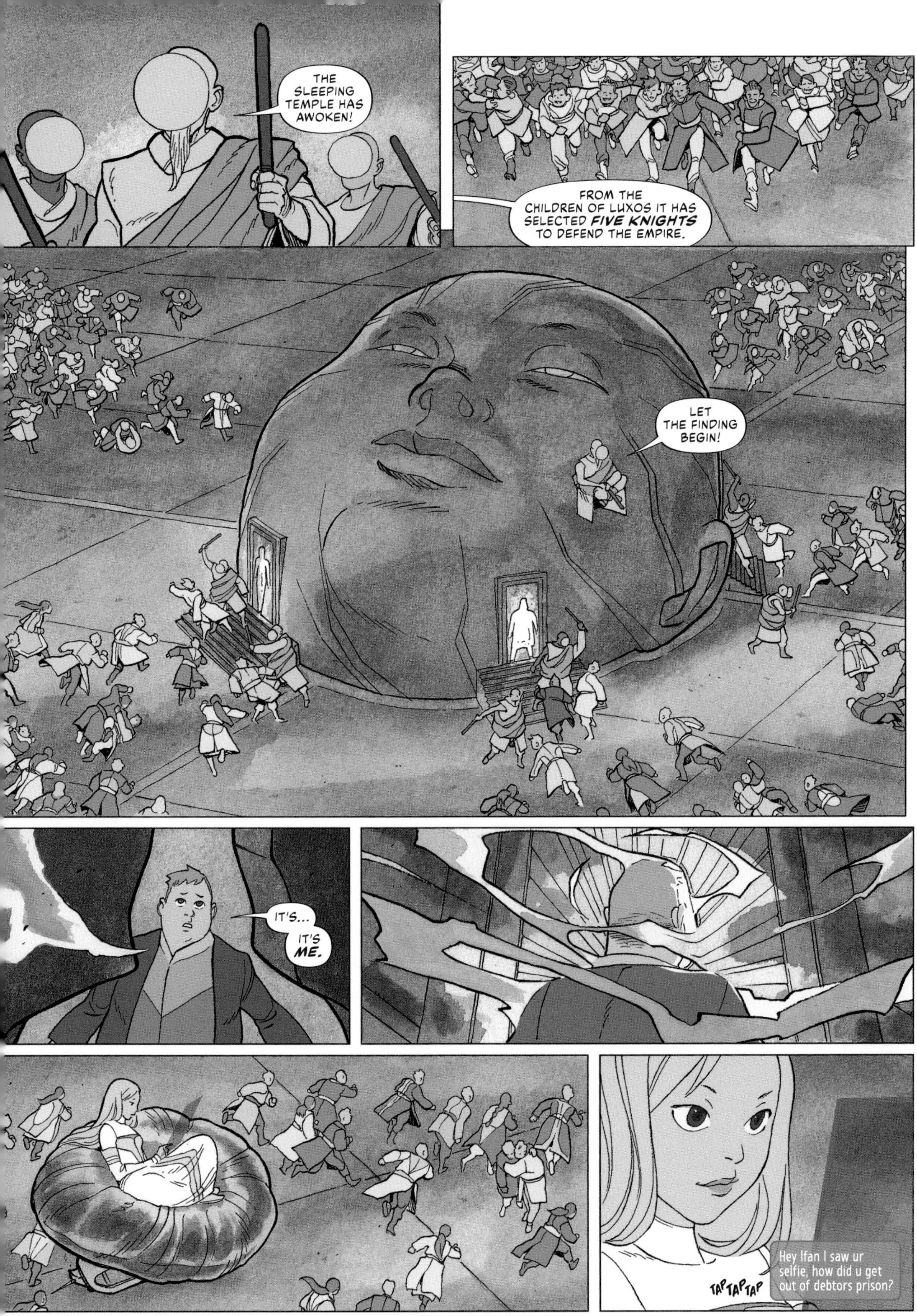
THE SLEEPING TEMPLE HAS AWOKEN!
FROM THE CHILDREN OF LUXOS IT HAS SELECTED **FIVE KNIGHTS** TO DEFEND THE EMPIRE.
LET THE FINDING BEGIN!
IT'S... IT'S **ME.**
TAP TAP TAP
Hey Ifan I saw ur selfie, how did u get out of debtors prison?

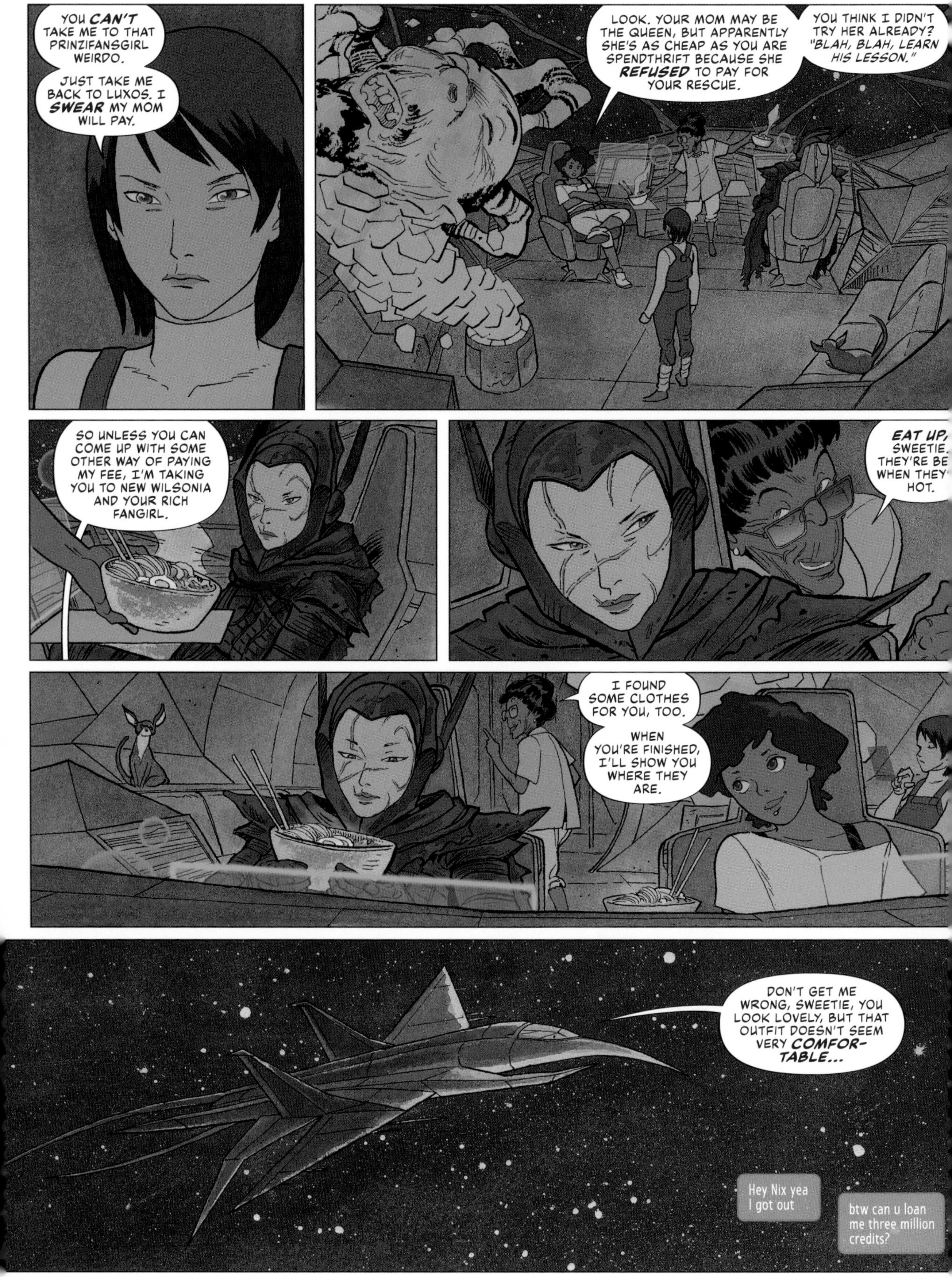
YOU CAN'T TAKE ME TO THAT PRINZIFANSGIRL WEIRDO.
JUST TAKE ME BACK TO LUXOS. I SWEAR MY MOM WILL PAY.
LOOK. YOUR MOM MAY BE THE QUEEN, BUT APPARENTLY SHE'S AS CHEAP AS YOU ARE SPENDTHRIFT BECAUSE SHE REFUSED TO PAY FOR YOUR RESCUE.
YOU THINK I DIDN'T TRY HER ALREADY? "BLAH, BLAH, LEARN HIS LESSON."
SO UNLESS YOU CAN COME UP WITH SOME OTHER WAY OF PAYING MY FEE, I'M TAKING YOU TO NEW WILSONIA AND YOUR RICH FANGIRL.
EAT UP, SWEETIE. THEY'RE BE WHEN THEY' HOT.
I FOUND SOME CLOTHES FOR YOU, TOO.
WHEN YOU'RE FINISHED, I'LL SHOW YOU WHERE THEY ARE.
DON'T GET ME WRONG, SWEETIE, YOU LOOK LOVELY, BUT THAT OUTFIT DOESN'T SEEM VERY COMFORTABLE...
Hey Nix yea I got out
btw can u loan me three million credits?

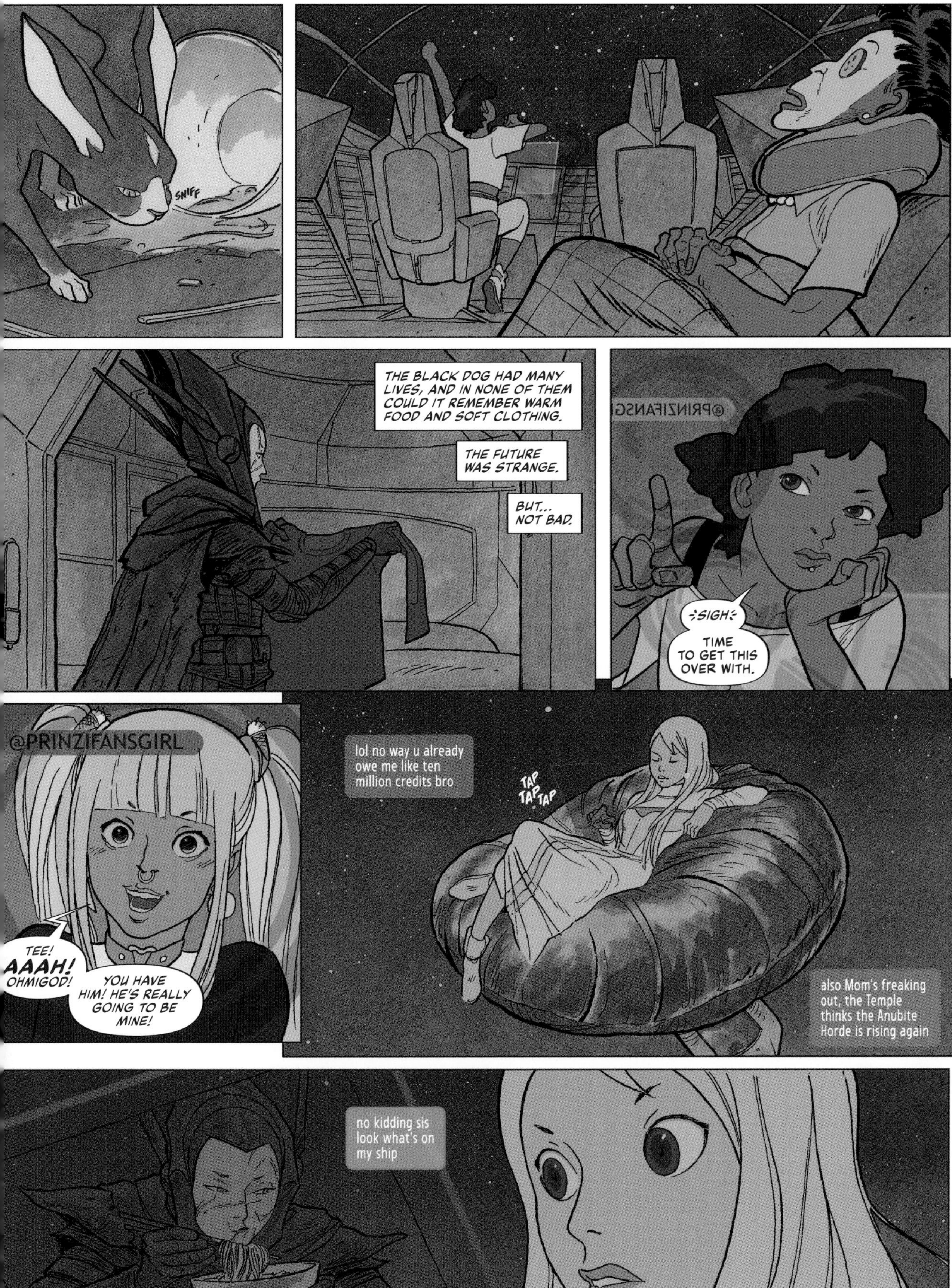
SNIFF
THE BLACK DOG HAD MANY LIVES, AND IN NONE OF THEM COULD IT REMEMBER WARM FOOD AND SOFT CLOTHING.
THE FUTURE WAS STRANGE.
BUT... NOT BAD.
@PRINZIFANSGI
-:-SIGH-:-
TIME TO GET THIS OVER WITH.
@PRINZIFANSGIRL
TEE! AAAH! OHMIGOD!
YOU HAVE HIM! HE'S REALLY GOING TO BE MINE!
lol no way u already owe me like ten million credits bro
TAP TAP TAP
also Mom's freaking out, the Temple thinks the Anubite Horde is rising again
no kidding sis look what's on my ship

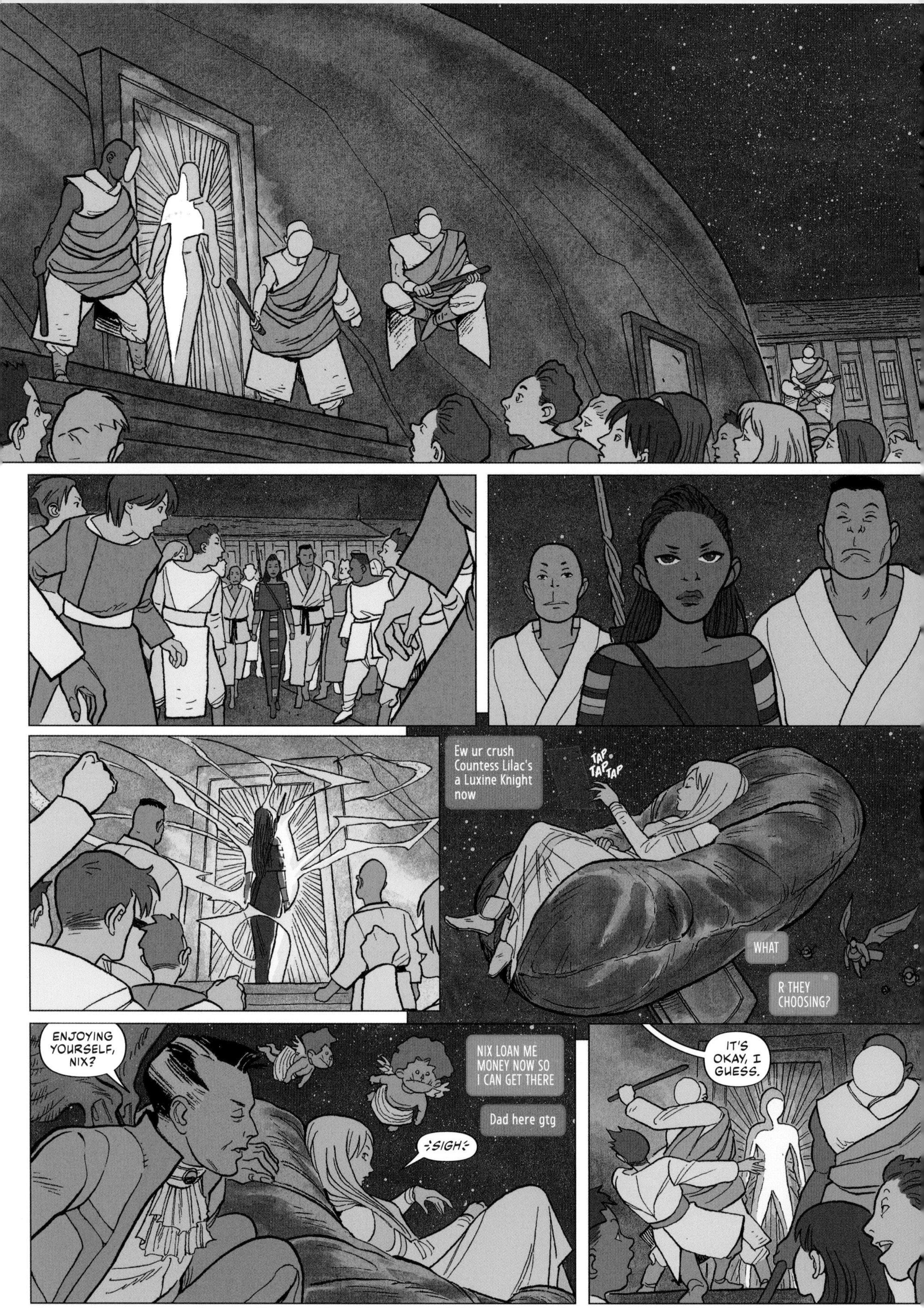
Ew ur crush Countess Lilac's a Luxine Knight now
TAP TAP TAP
WHAT
R THEY CHOOSING?
ENJOYING YOURSELF, NIX?
NIX LOAN ME MONEY NOW SO I CAN GET THERE
Dad here gtg
SIGH
IT'S OKAY, I GUESS.

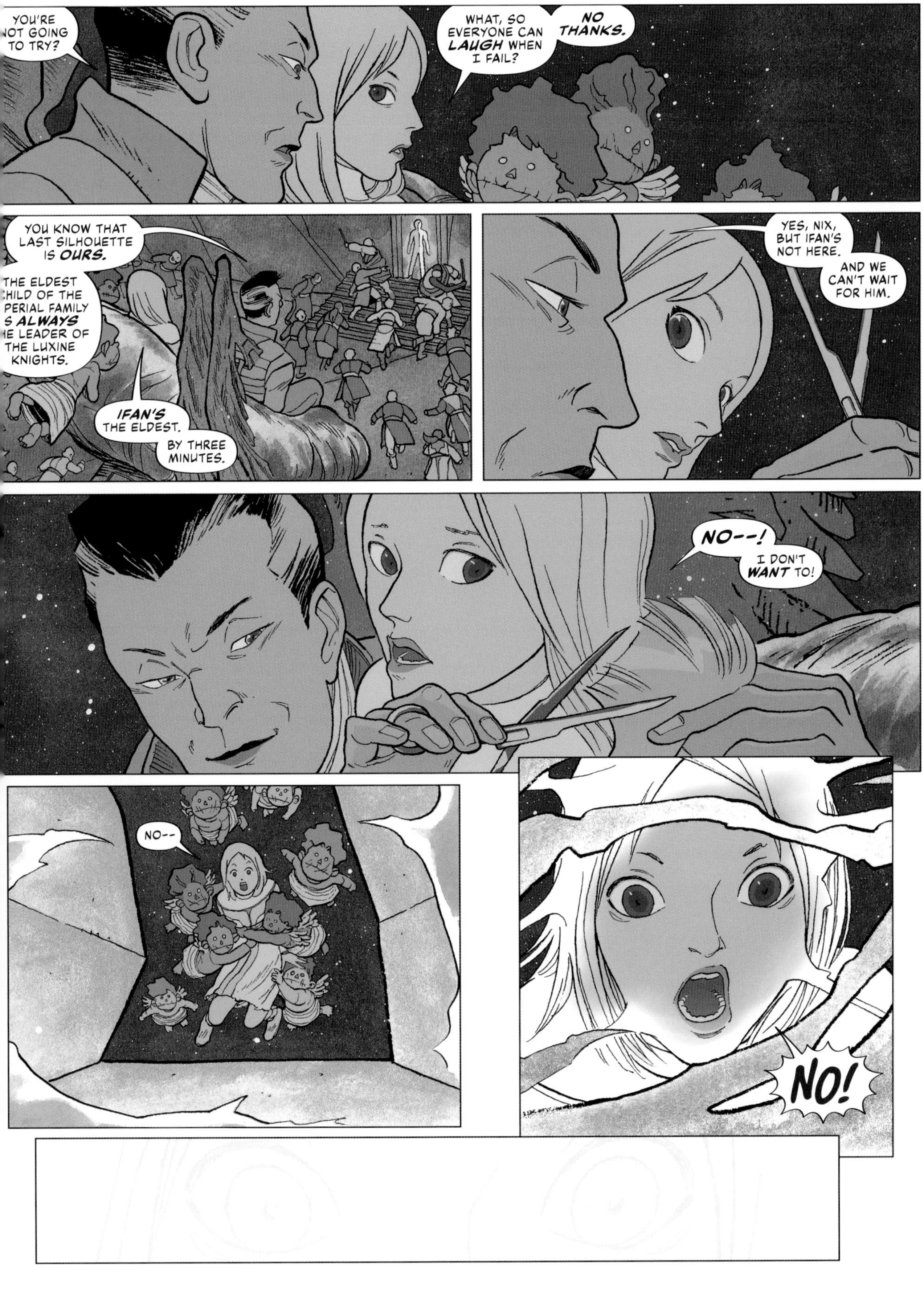

YOU'RE NOT GOING TO TRY?
WHAT, SO EVERYONE CAN LAUGH WHEN I FAIL?
NO THANKS.
YOU KNOW THAT LAST SILHOUETTE IS OURS.
THE ELDEST CHILD OF THE PERIAL FAMILY S ALWAYS HE LEADER OF THE LUXINE KNIGHTS.
IFAN'S THE ELDEST.
BY THREE MINUTES.
YES, NIX, BUT IFAN'S NOT HERE.
AND WE CAN'T WAIT FOR HIM.
NO--!
I DON'T WANT TO!
NO--
NO!

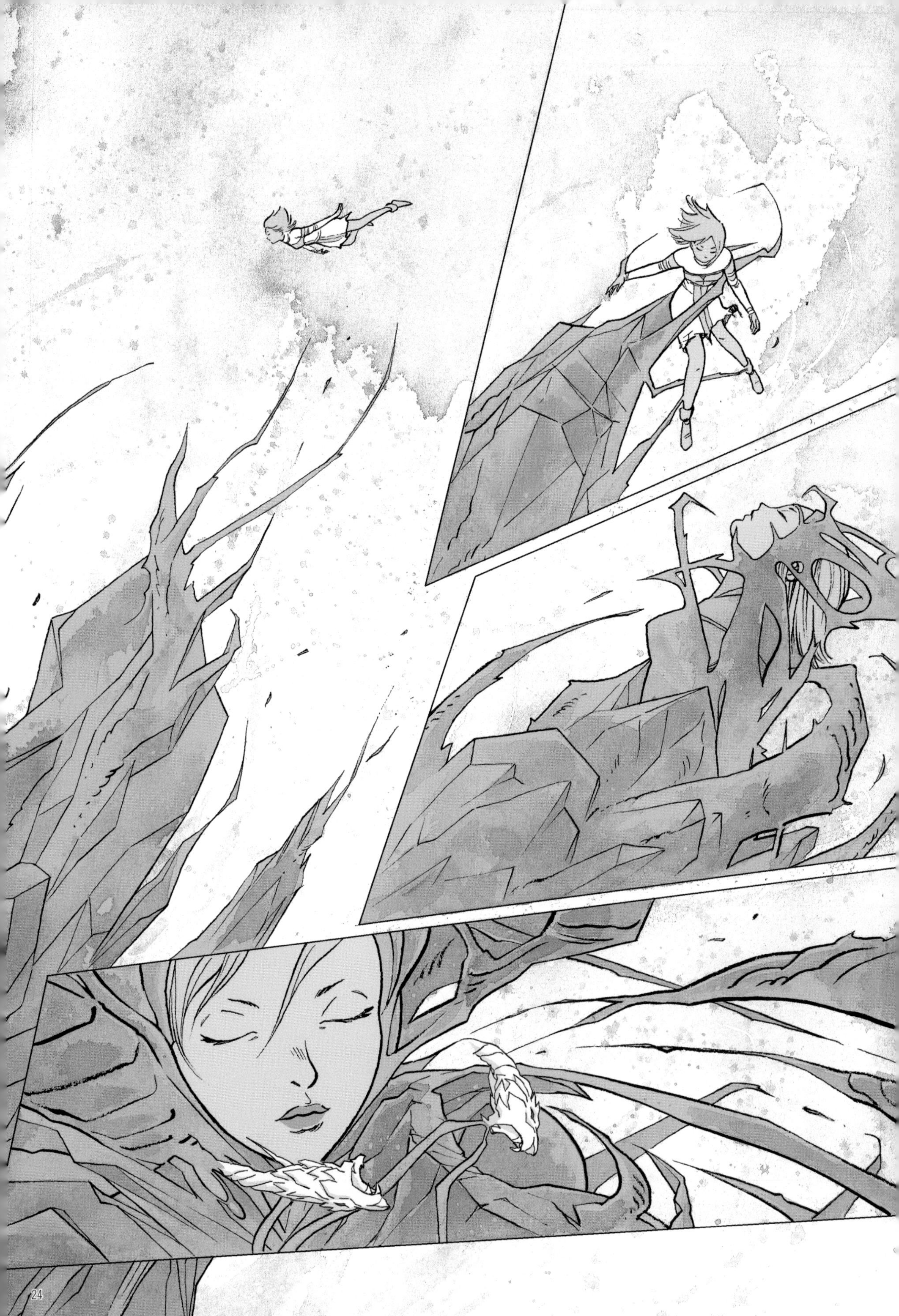

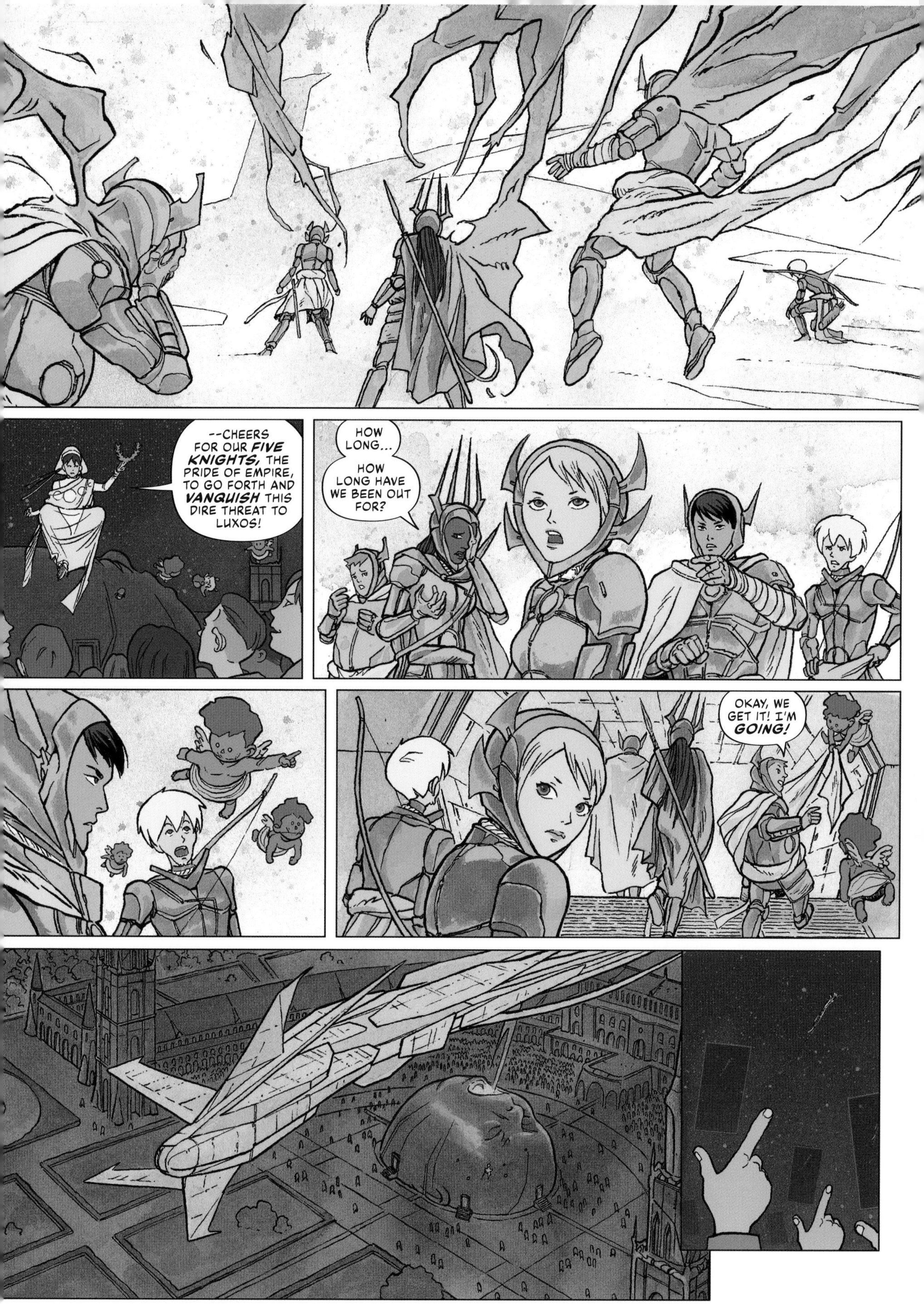
--CHEERS FOR OUR FIVE KNIGHTS, THE PRIDE OF EMPIRE, TO GO FORTH AND VANQUISH THIS DIRE THREAT TO LUXOS!
HOW LONG...
HOW LONG HAVE WE BEEN OUT FOR?
OKAY, WE GET IT! I'M GOING!

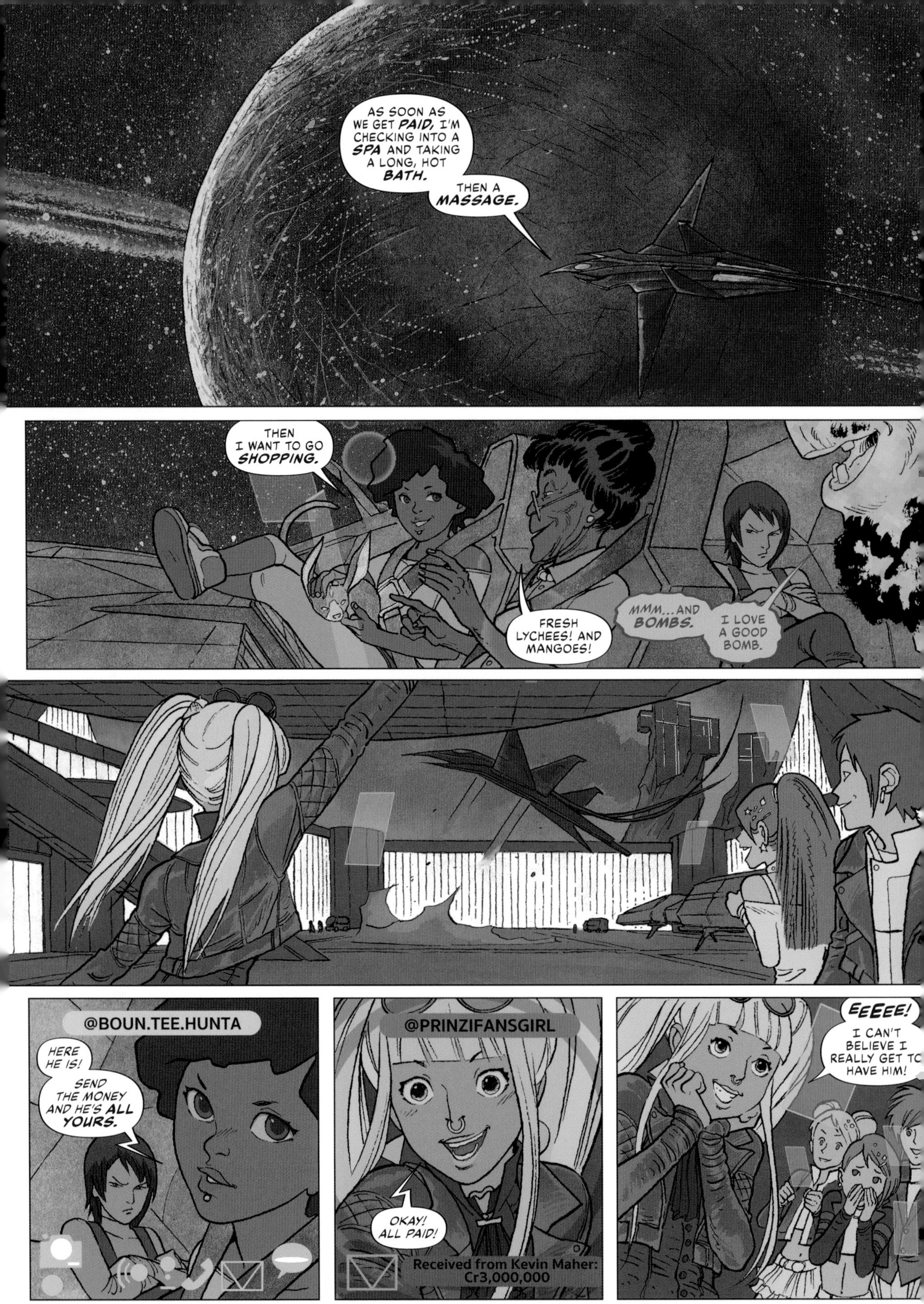

AS SOON AS WE GET PAID, I'M CHECKING INTO A SPA AND TAKING A LONG, HOT BATH.
THEN A MASSAGE.
THEN I WANT TO GO SHOPPING.
FRESH LYCHEES! AND MANGOES!
MMM...AND BOMBS.
I LOVE A GOOD BOMB.
@BOUN.TEE.HUNTA
HERE HE IS!
SEND THE MONEY AND HE'S ALL YOURS.
@PRINZIFANSGIRL
OKAY! ALL PAID!
Received from Kevin Maher: Cr3,000,000
EEEEE!
I CAN'T BELIEVE I REALLY GET TO HAVE HIM!

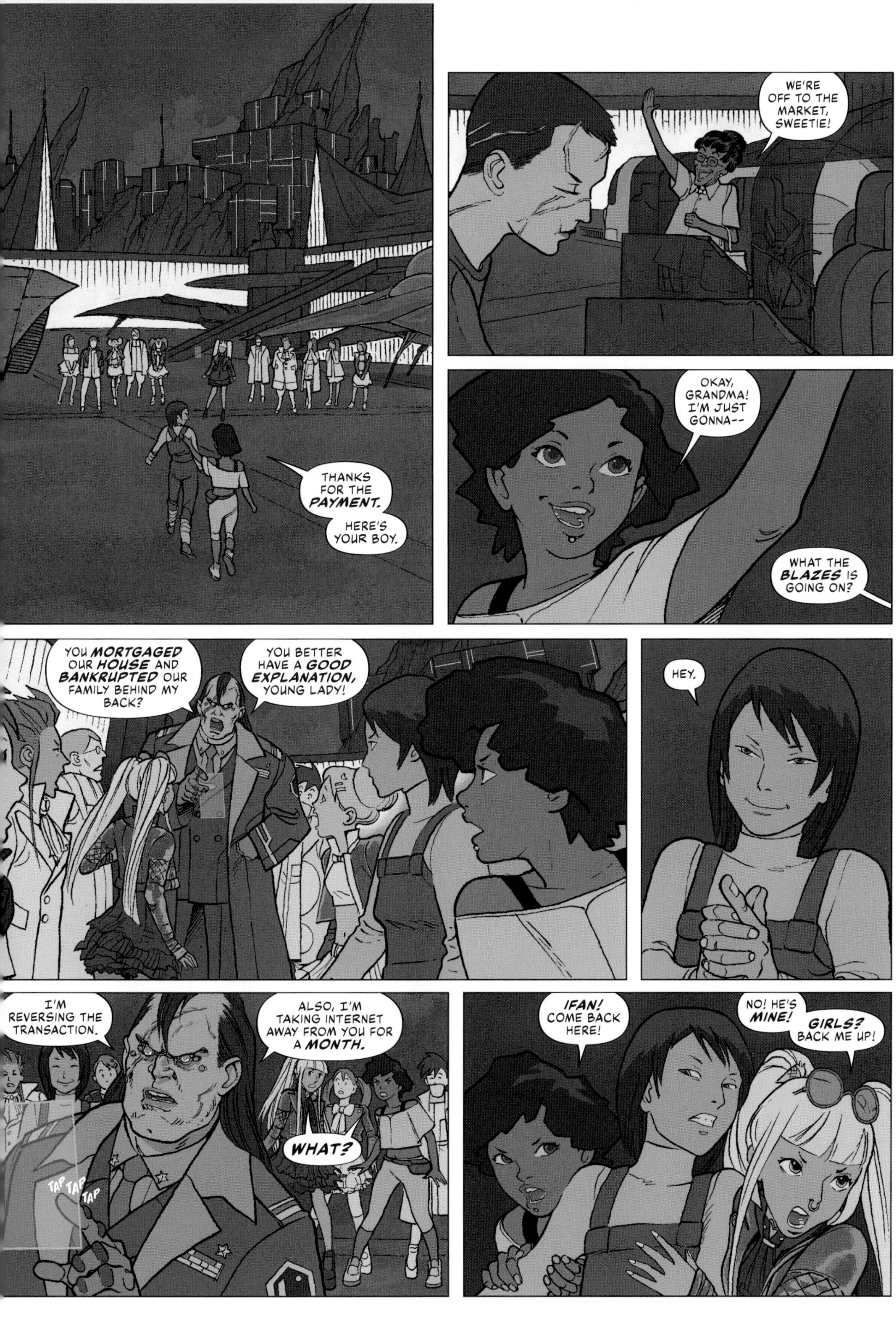
THANKS FOR THE PAYMENT.
HERE'S YOUR BOY.
WE'RE OFF TO THE MARKET, SWEETIE!
OKAY, GRANDMA! I'M JUST GONNA--
WHAT THE BLAZES IS GOING ON?
YOU MORTGAGED OUR HOUSE AND BANKRUPTED OUR FAMILY BEHIND MY BACK?
YOU BETTER HAVE A GOOD EXPLANATION, YOUNG LADY!
HEY.
I'M REVERSING THE TRANSACTION.
ALSO, I'M TAKING INTERNET AWAY FROM YOU FOR A MONTH.
WHAT?
TAP TAP TAP
IFAN! COME BACK HERE!
NO! HE'S MINE!
GIRLS? BACK ME UP!

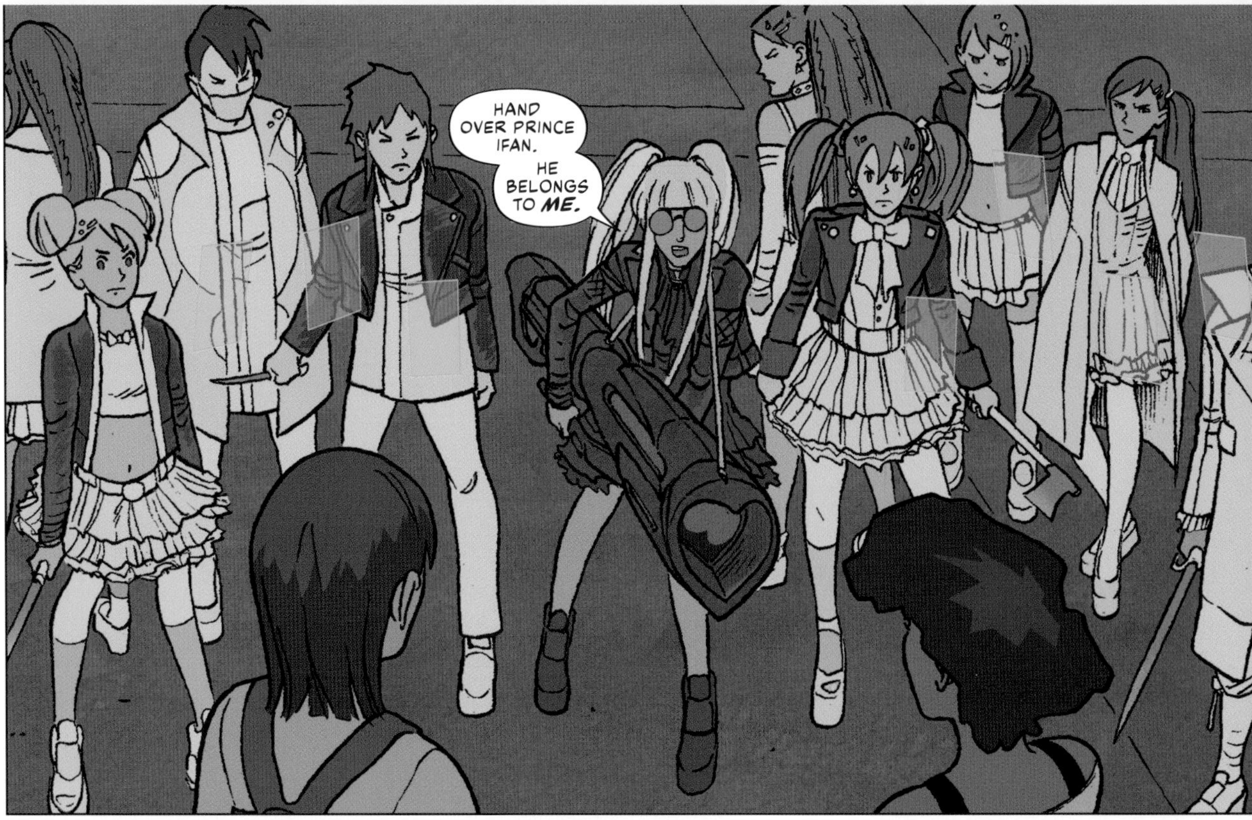
HAND OVER PRINCE IFAN.
HE BELONGS TO *ME.*

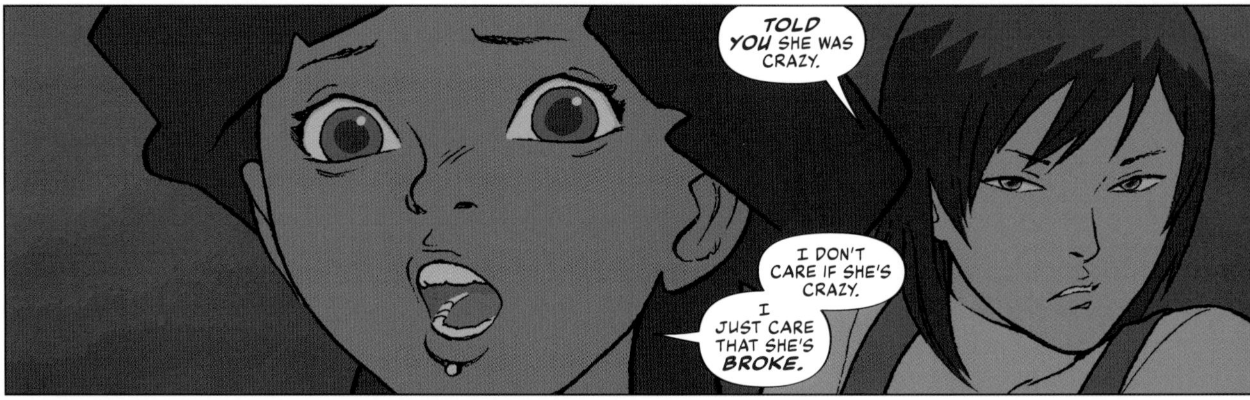
TOLD YOU SHE WAS CRAZY.
I DON'T CARE IF SHE'S CRAZY.
I JUST CARE THAT SHE'S *BROKE.*

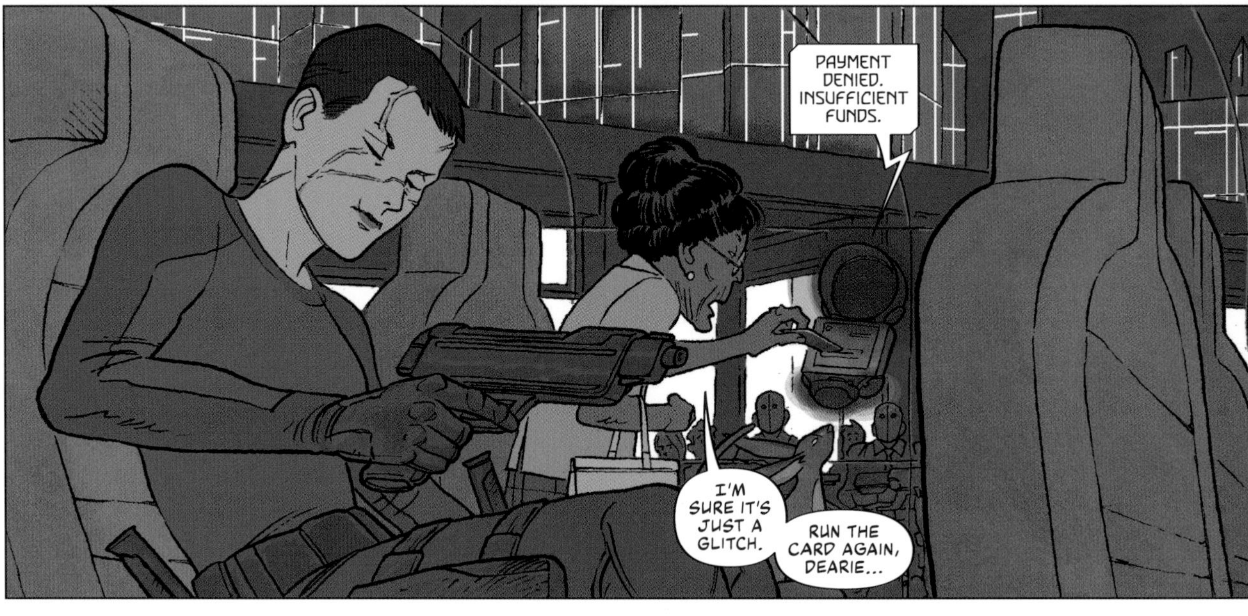
PAYMENT DENIED. INSUFFICIENT FUNDS.
I'M SURE IT'S JUST A GLITCH.
RUN THE CARD AGAIN, DEARIE...

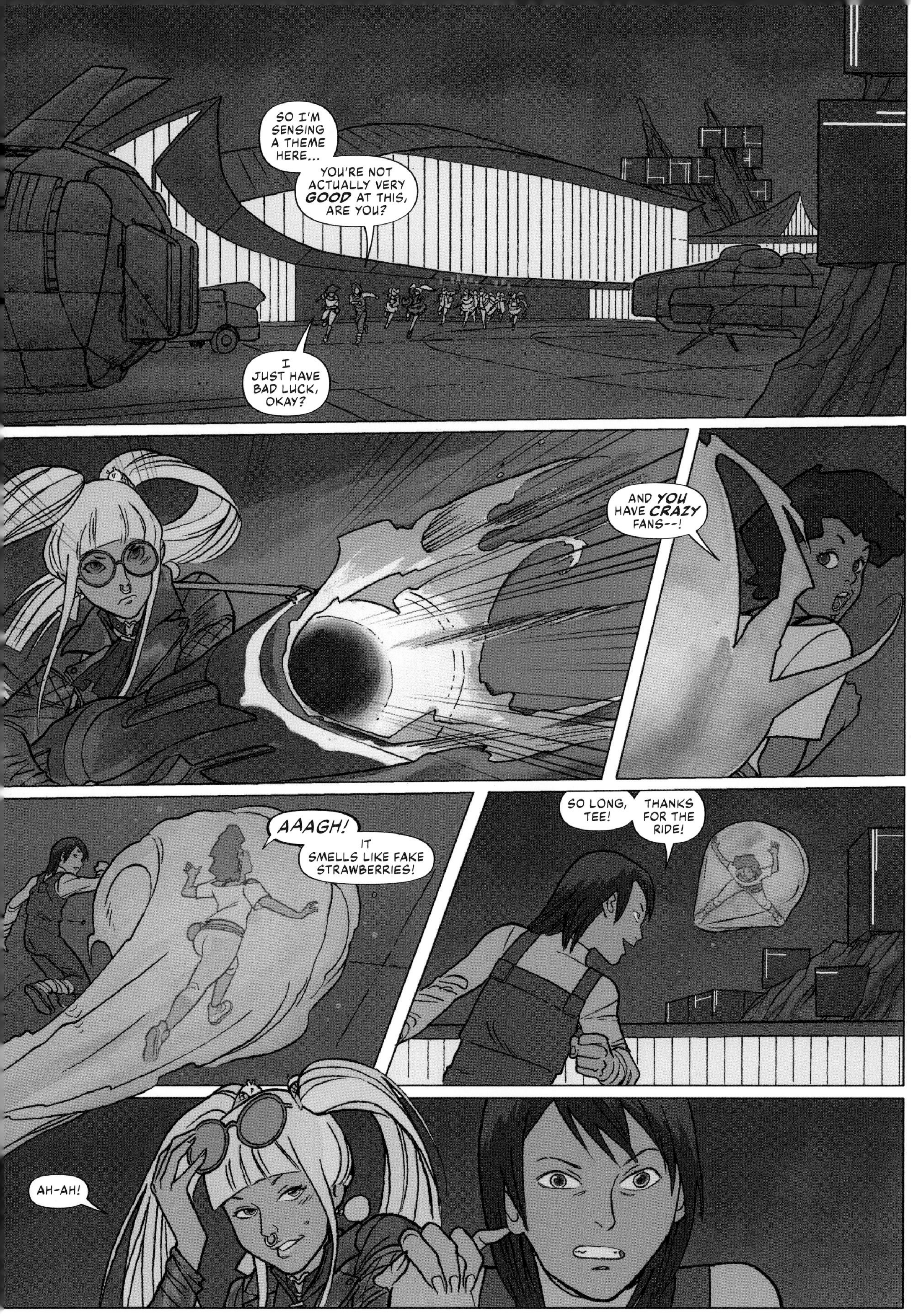
SO I'M SENSING A THEME HERE...
YOU'RE NOT ACTUALLY VERY GOOD AT THIS, ARE YOU?
I JUST HAVE BAD LUCK, OKAY?
AND YOU HAVE CRAZY FANS--!
AAAGH!
IT SMELLS LIKE FAKE STRAWBERRIES!
SO LONG, TEE!
THANKS FOR THE RIDE!
AH-AH!

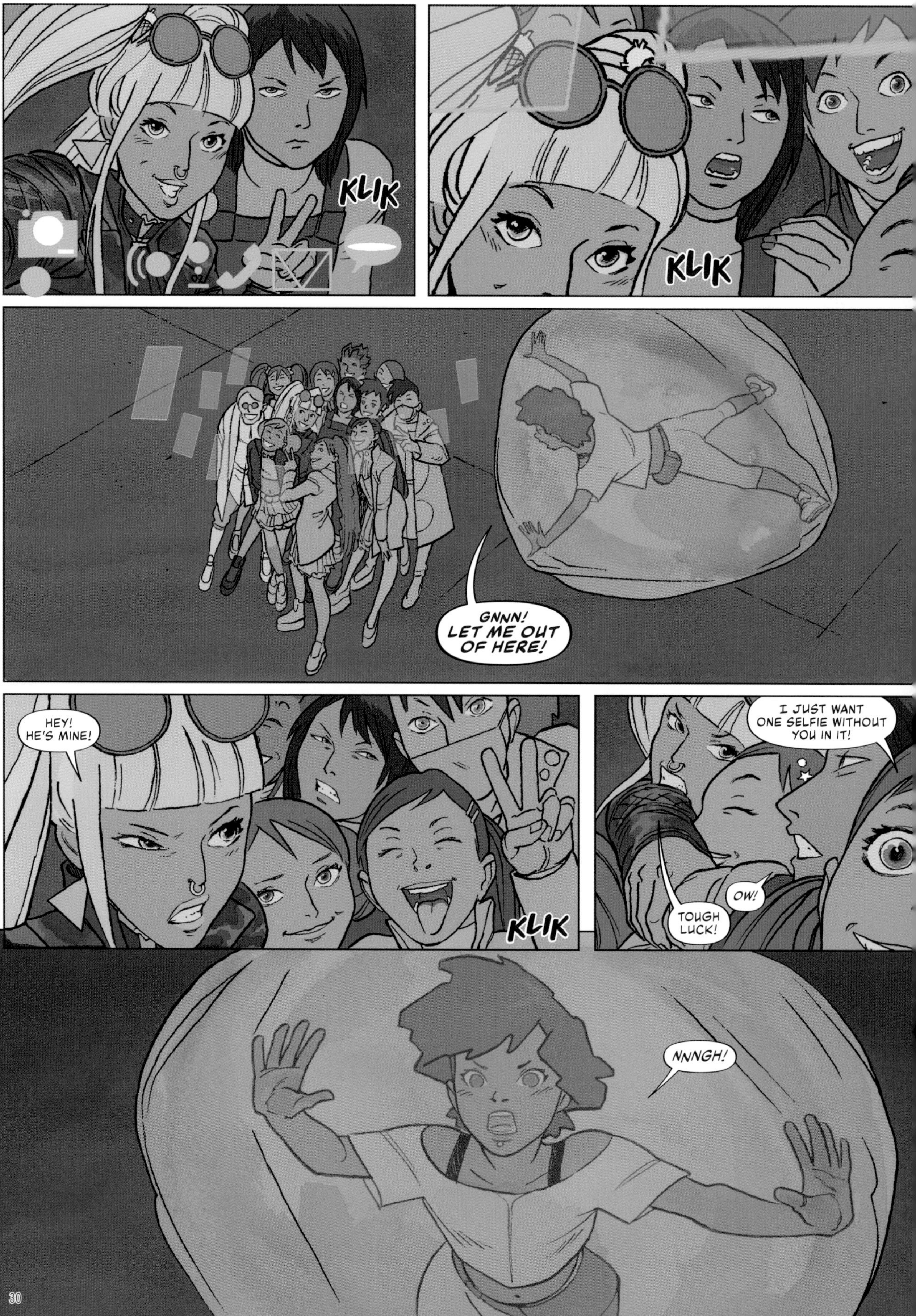

KLIK
KLIK
GNNN! LET ME OUT OF HERE!
HEY! HE'S MINE!
KLIK
I JUST WANT ONE SELFIE WITHOUT YOU IN IT!
TOUGH LUCK!
OW!
NNNGH!

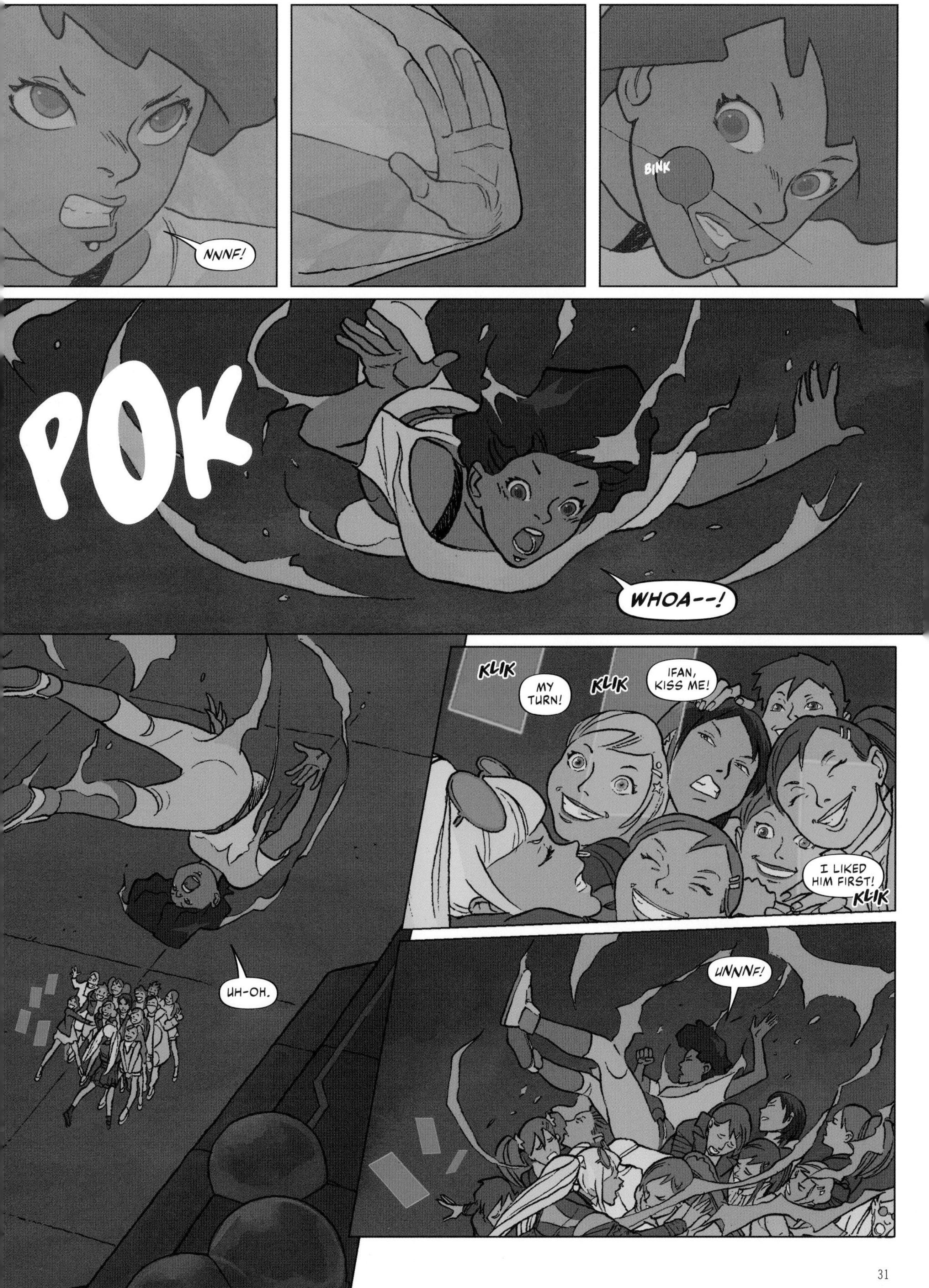

NNNF!
BINK
POK
WHOA--!
KLIK
MY TURN!
KLIK
IFAN, KISS ME!
I LIKED HIM FIRST!
KLIK
UH-OH.
UNNNF!

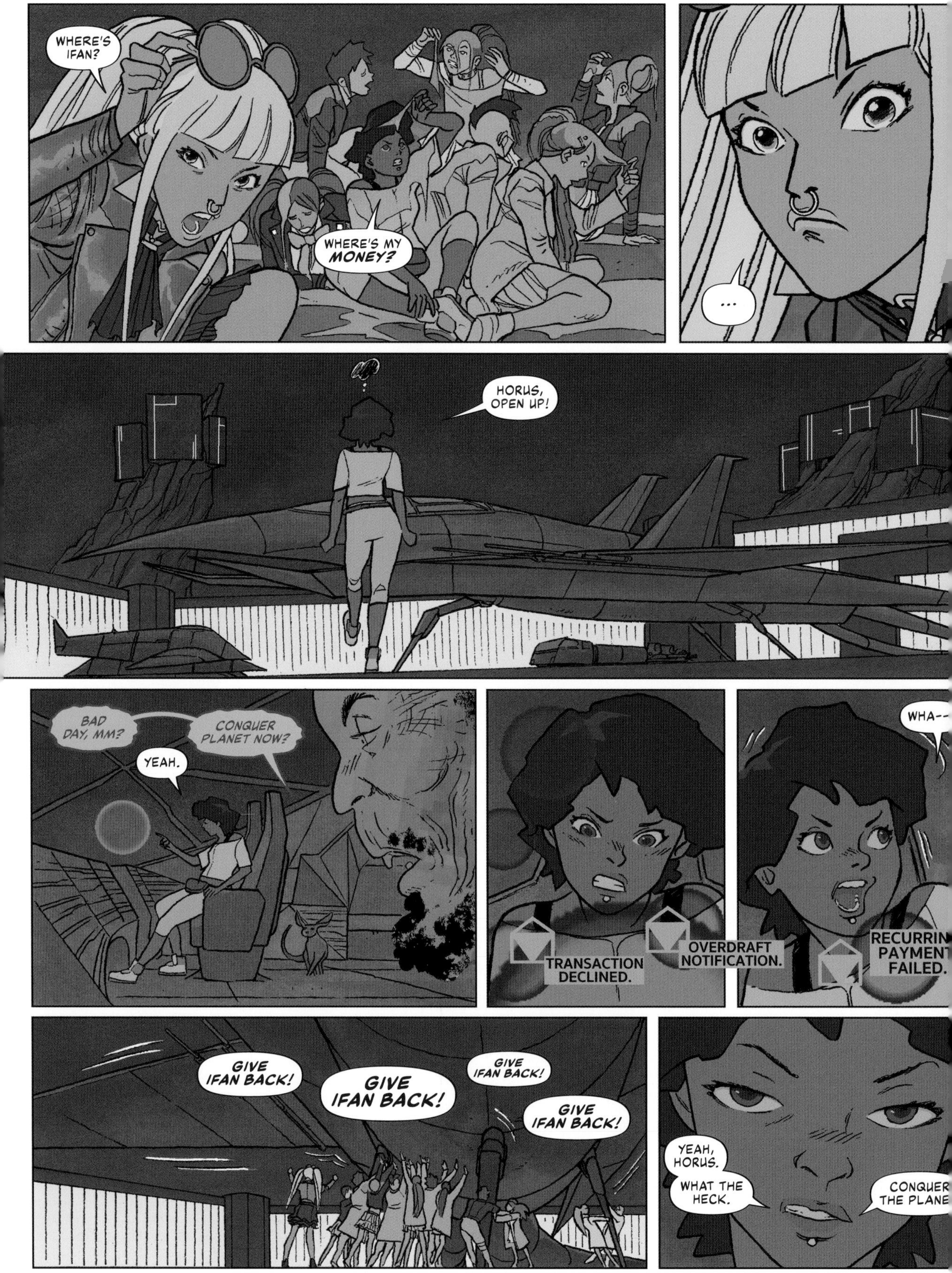
WHERE'S IFAN?
WHERE'S MY MONEY?
...
HORUS, OPEN UP!
BAD DAY, MM?
CONQUER PLANET NOW?
YEAH.
TRANSACTION DECLINED.
OVERDRAFT NOTIFICATION.
WHA--
RECURRIN PAYMENT FAILED.
GIVE IFAN BACK!
GIVE IFAN BACK!
GIVE IFAN BACK!
GIVE IFAN BACK!
YEAH, HORUS.
WHAT THE HECK.
CONQUER THE PLANE

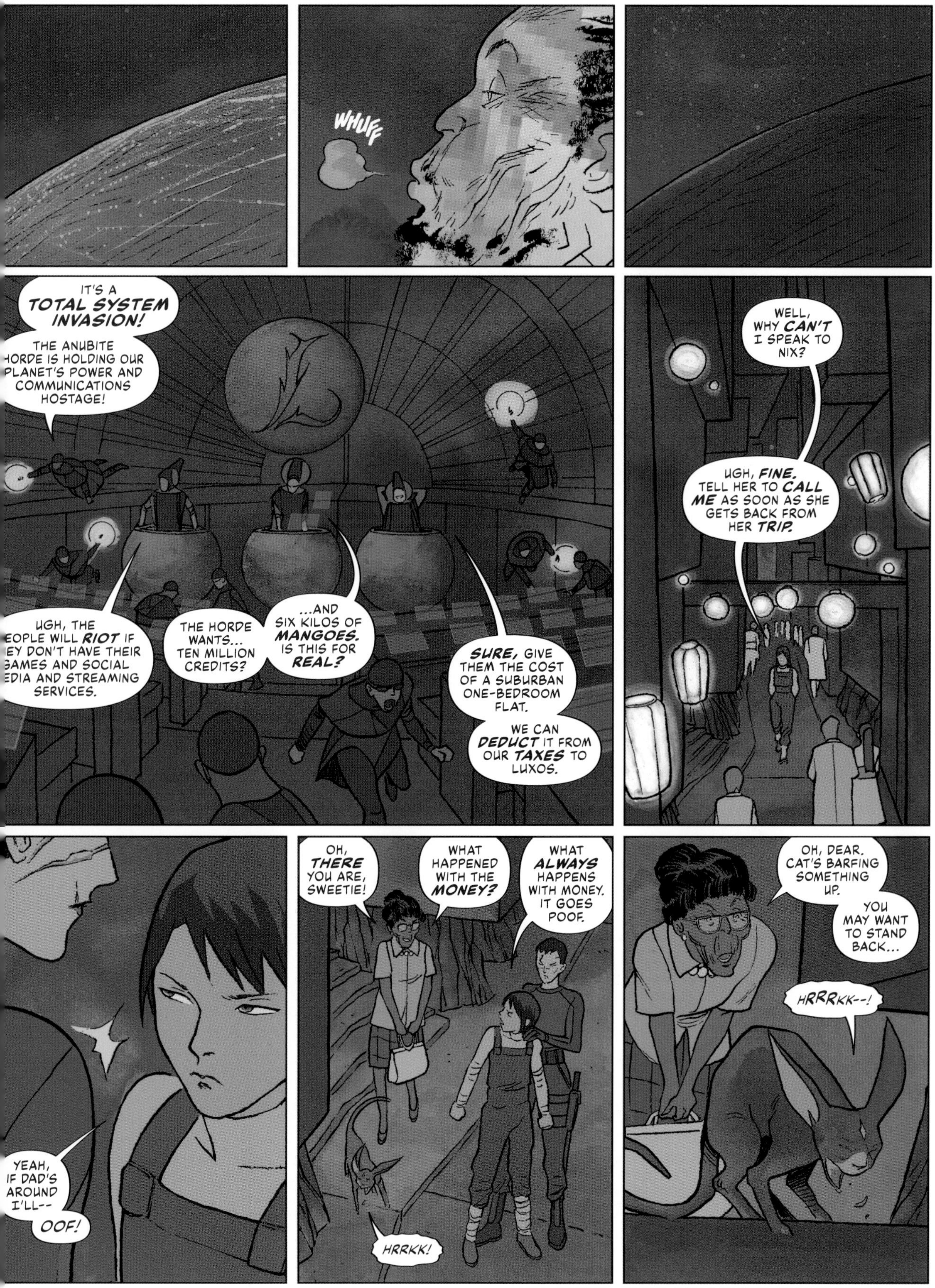
WHUFF
IT'S A TOTAL SYSTEM INVASION!
THE ANUBITE HORDE IS HOLDING OUR PLANET'S POWER AND COMMUNICATIONS HOSTAGE!
UGH, THE EOPLE WILL RIOT IF EY DON'T HAVE THEIR GAMES AND SOCIAL EDIA AND STREAMING SERVICES.
THE HORDE WANTS... TEN MILLION CREDITS?
...AND SIX KILOS OF MANGOES. IS THIS FOR REAL?
SURE, GIVE THEM THE COST OF A SUBURBAN ONE-BEDROOM FLAT.
WE CAN DEDUCT IT FROM OUR TAXES TO LUXOS.
WELL, WHY CAN'T I SPEAK TO NIX?
UGH, FINE. TELL HER TO CALL ME AS SOON AS SHE GETS BACK FROM HER TRIP.
YEAH, IF DAD'S AROUND I'LL--
OOF!
OH, THERE YOU ARE, SWEETIE!
WHAT HAPPENED WITH THE MONEY?
WHAT ALWAYS HAPPENS WITH MONEY. IT GOES POOF.
HRRKK!
OH, DEAR. CAT'S BARFING SOMETHING UP.
YOU MAY WANT TO STAND BACK...
HRRRKK--!

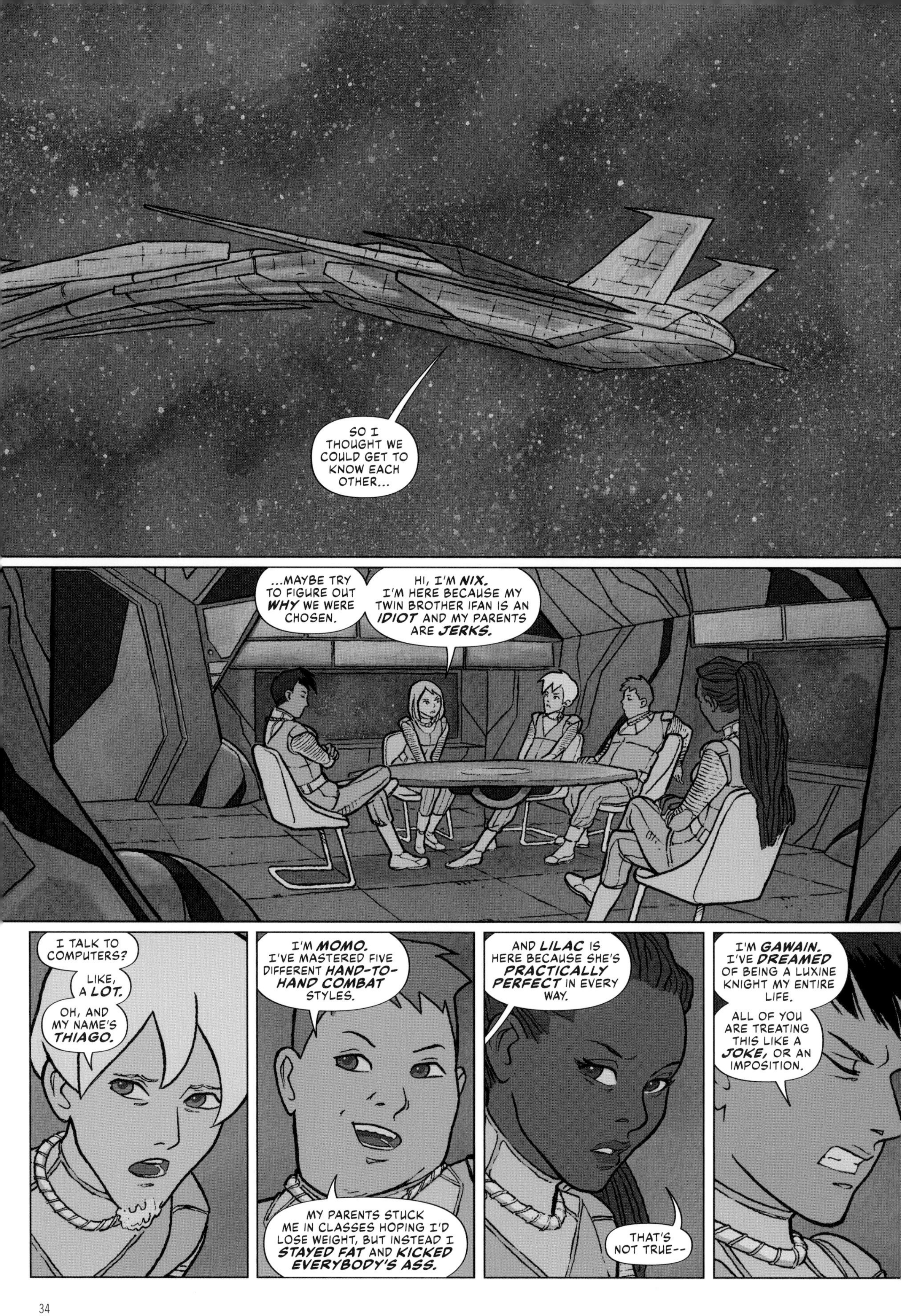

SO I THOUGHT WE COULD GET TO KNOW EACH OTHER...
...MAYBE TRY TO FIGURE OUT WHY WE WERE CHOSEN.
HI, I'M NIX. I'M HERE BECAUSE MY TWIN BROTHER IFAN IS AN IDIOT AND MY PARENTS ARE JERKS.
I TALK TO COMPUTERS?
LIKE, A LOT.
OH, AND MY NAME'S THIAGO.
I'M MOMO. I'VE MASTERED FIVE DIFFERENT HAND-TO-HAND COMBAT STYLES.
MY PARENTS STUCK ME IN CLASSES HOPING I'D LOSE WEIGHT, BUT INSTEAD I STAYED FAT AND KICKED EVERYBODY'S ASS.
AND LILAC IS HERE BECAUSE SHE'S PRACTICALLY PERFECT IN EVERY WAY.
THAT'S NOT TRUE--
I'M GAWAIN. I'VE DREAMED OF BEING A LUXINE KNIGHT MY ENTIRE LIFE.
ALL OF YOU ARE TREATING THIS LIKE A JOKE, OR AN IMPOSITION.

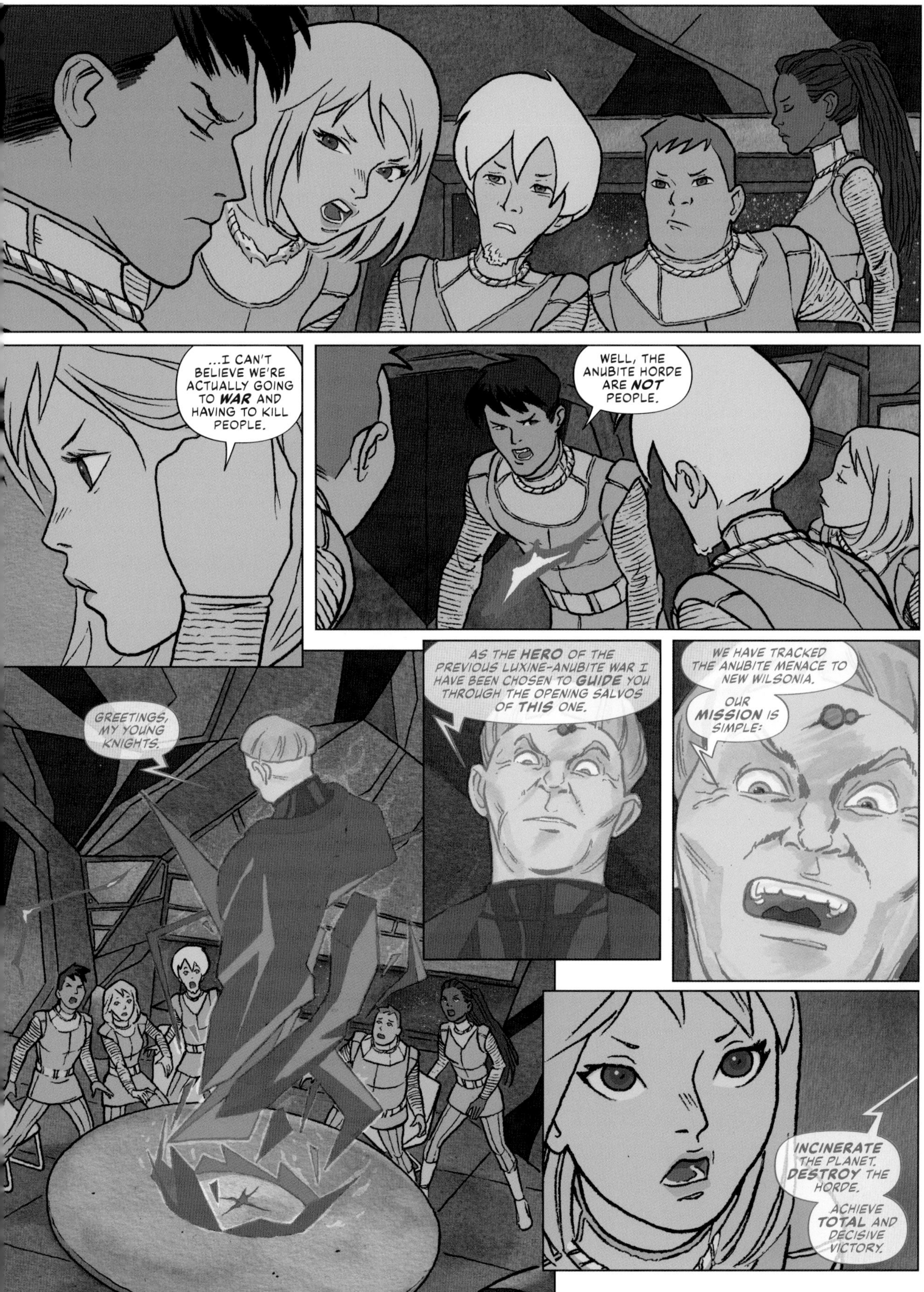

...I CAN'T BELIEVE WE'RE ACTUALLY GOING TO WAR AND HAVING TO KILL PEOPLE.
WELL, THE ANUBITE HORDE ARE NOT PEOPLE.
GREETINGS, MY YOUNG KNIGHTS.
AS THE HERO OF THE PREVIOUS LUXINE-ANUBITE WAR I HAVE BEEN CHOSEN TO GUIDE YOU THROUGH THE OPENING SALVOS OF THIS ONE.
WE HAVE TRACKED THE ANUBITE MENACE TO NEW WILSONIA.
OUR MISSION IS SIMPLE:
INCINERATE THE PLANET. DESTROY THE HORDE.
ACHIEVE TOTAL AND DECISIVE VICTORY.

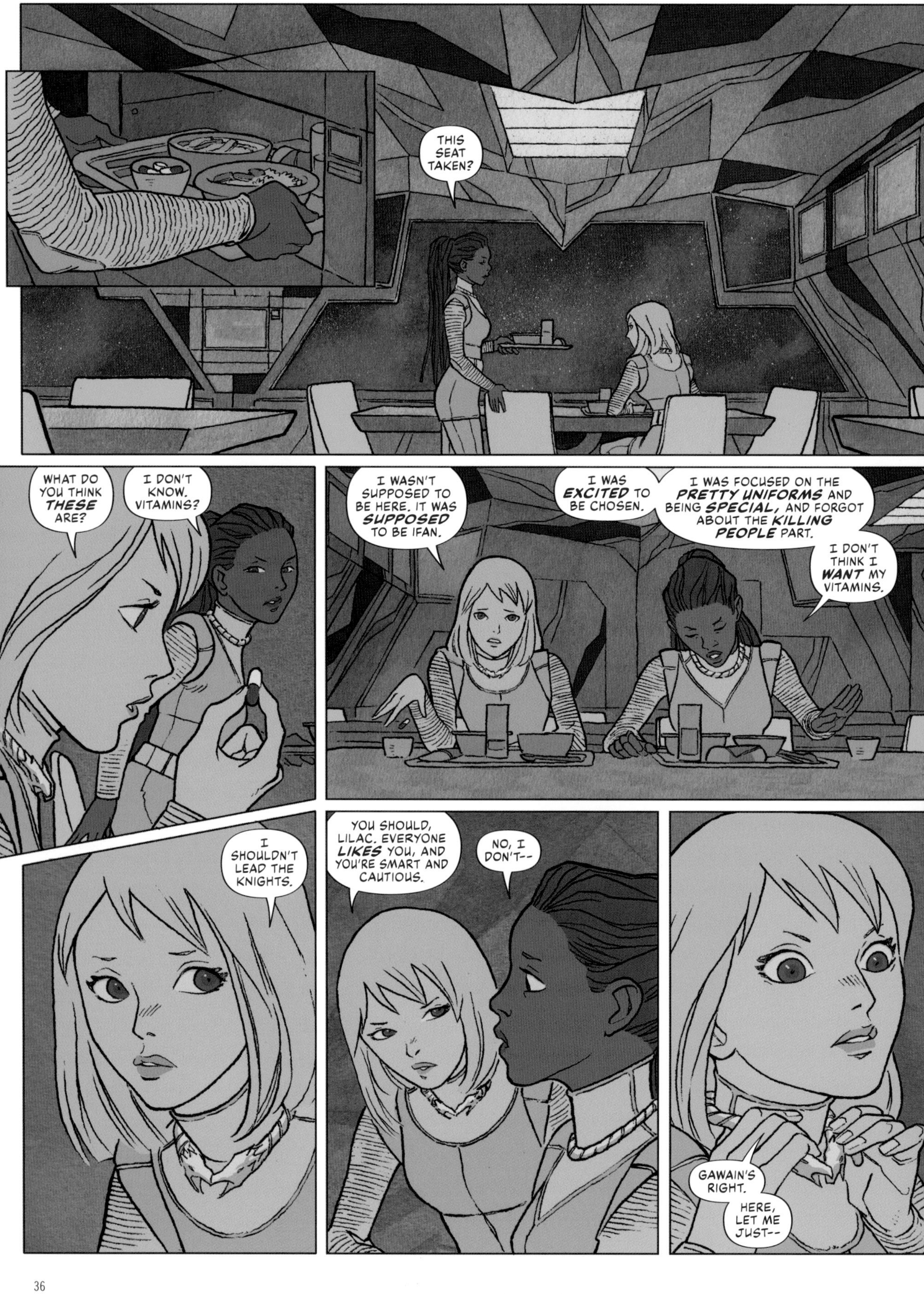
THIS SEAT TAKEN?
WHAT DO YOU THINK *THESE* ARE?
I DON'T KNOW. VITAMINS?
I WASN'T SUPPOSED TO BE HERE. IT WAS *SUPPOSED* TO BE IFAN.
I WAS *EXCITED* TO BE CHOSEN.
I WAS FOCUSED ON THE *PRETTY UNIFORMS* AND BEING *SPECIAL,* AND FORGOT ABOUT THE *KILLING PEOPLE* PART.
I DON'T THINK I *WANT* MY VITAMINS.
I SHOULDN'T LEAD THE KNIGHTS.
YOU SHOULD, LILAC. EVERYONE *LIKES* YOU, AND YOU'RE SMART AND CAUTIOUS.
NO, I DON'T--
GAWAIN'S RIGHT.
HERE, LET ME JUST--

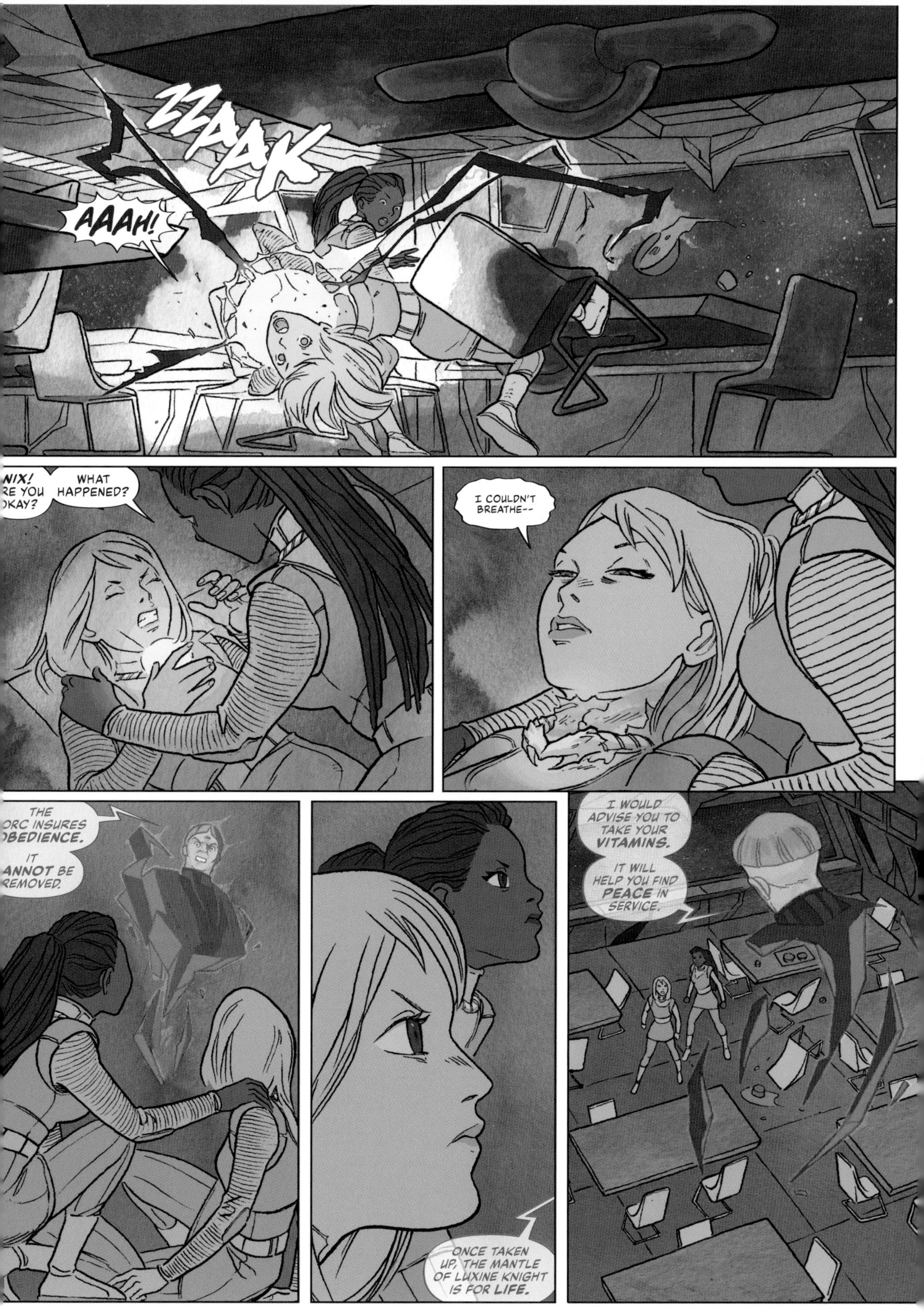
ZZAPAK
AAAH!
NIX! RE YOU OKAY?
WHAT HAPPENED?
I COULDN'T BREATHE--
THE ORC INSURES OBEDIENCE.
IT ANNOT BE REMOVED.
ONCE TAKEN UP, THE MANTLE OF LUXINE KNIGHT IS FOR LIFE.
I WOULD ADVISE YOU TO TAKE YOUR VITAMINS.
IT WILL HELP YOU FIND PEACE IN SERVICE.

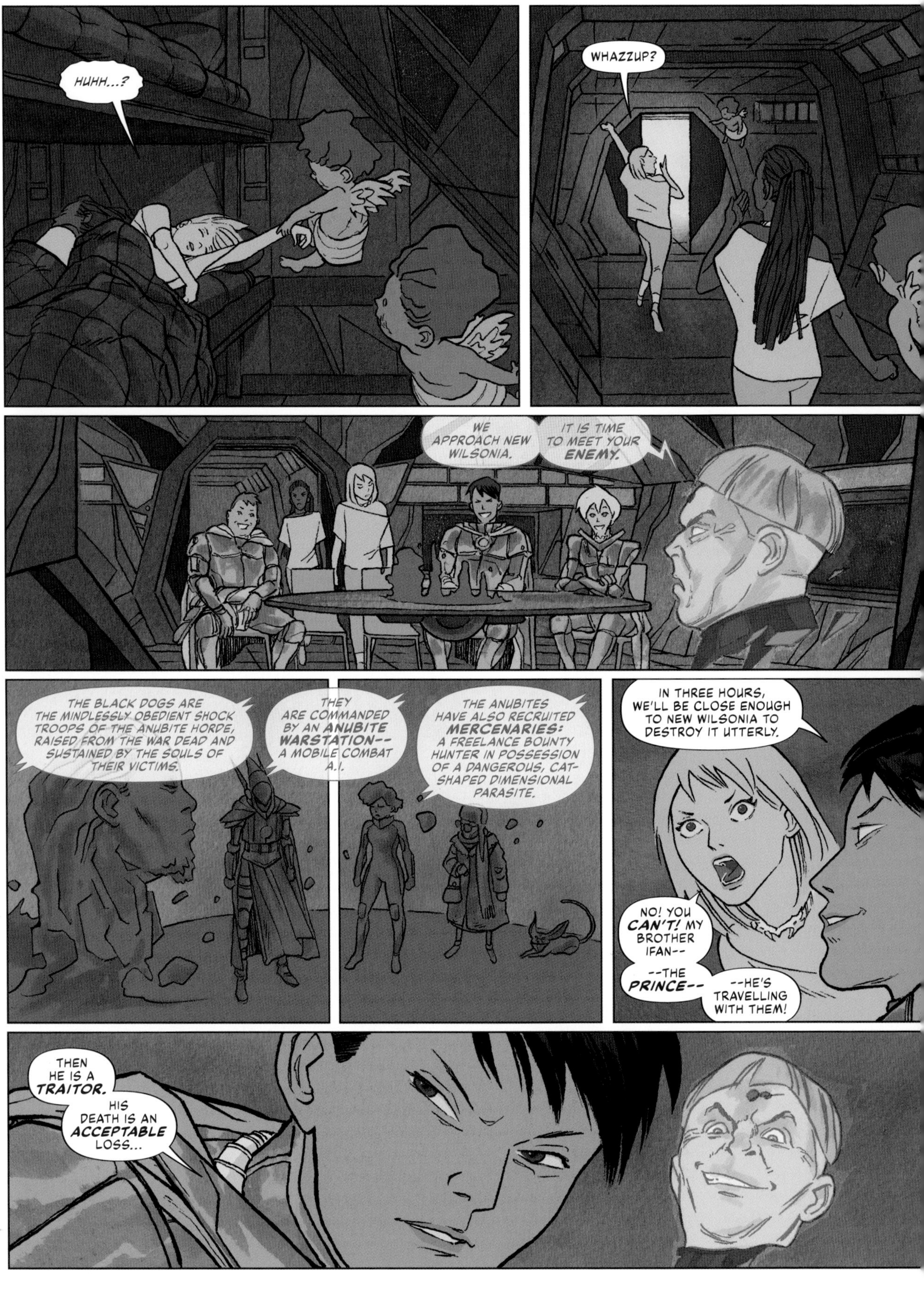
HUHH...?
WHAZZUP?
WE APPROACH NEW WILSONIA.
IT IS TIME TO MEET YOUR ENEMY.
THE BLACK DOGS ARE THE MINDLESSLY OBEDIENT SHOCK TROOPS OF THE ANUBITE HORDE, RAISED FROM THE WAR DEAD AND SUSTAINED BY THE SOULS OF THEIR VICTIMS.
THEY ARE COMMANDED BY AN ANUBITE WARSTATION-- A MOBILE COMBAT A.I.
THE ANUBITES HAVE ALSO RECRUITED MERCENARIES: A FREELANCE BOUNTY HUNTER IN POSSESSION OF A DANGEROUS, CAT-SHAPED DIMENSIONAL PARASITE.
IN THREE HOURS, WE'LL BE CLOSE ENOUGH TO NEW WILSONIA TO DESTROY IT UTTERLY.
NO! YOU CAN'T! MY BROTHER IFAN--
--THE PRINCE--
--HE'S TRAVELLING WITH THEM!
THEN HE IS A TRAITOR.
HIS DEATH IS AN ACCEPTABLE LOSS...

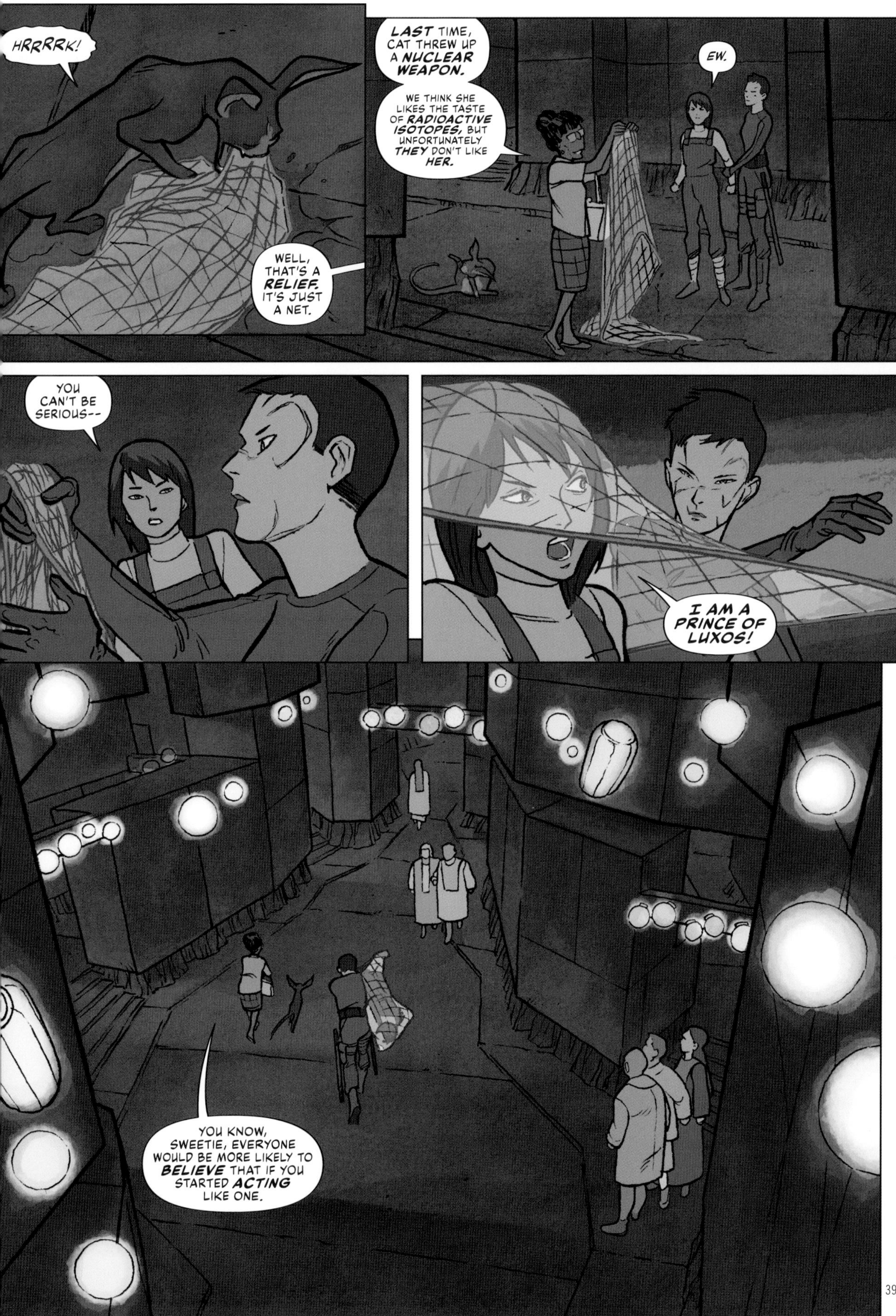

HRRRRK!
WELL, THAT'S A RELIEF. IT'S JUST A NET.
LAST TIME, CAT THREW UP A NUCLEAR WEAPON.
WE THINK SHE LIKES THE TASTE OF RADIOACTIVE ISOTOPES, BUT UNFORTUNATELY THEY DON'T LIKE HER.
EW.
YOU CAN'T BE SERIOUS--
I AM A PRINCE OF LUXOS!
YOU KNOW, SWEETIE, EVERYONE WOULD BE MORE LIKELY TO BELIEVE THAT IF YOU STARTED ACTING LIKE ONE.

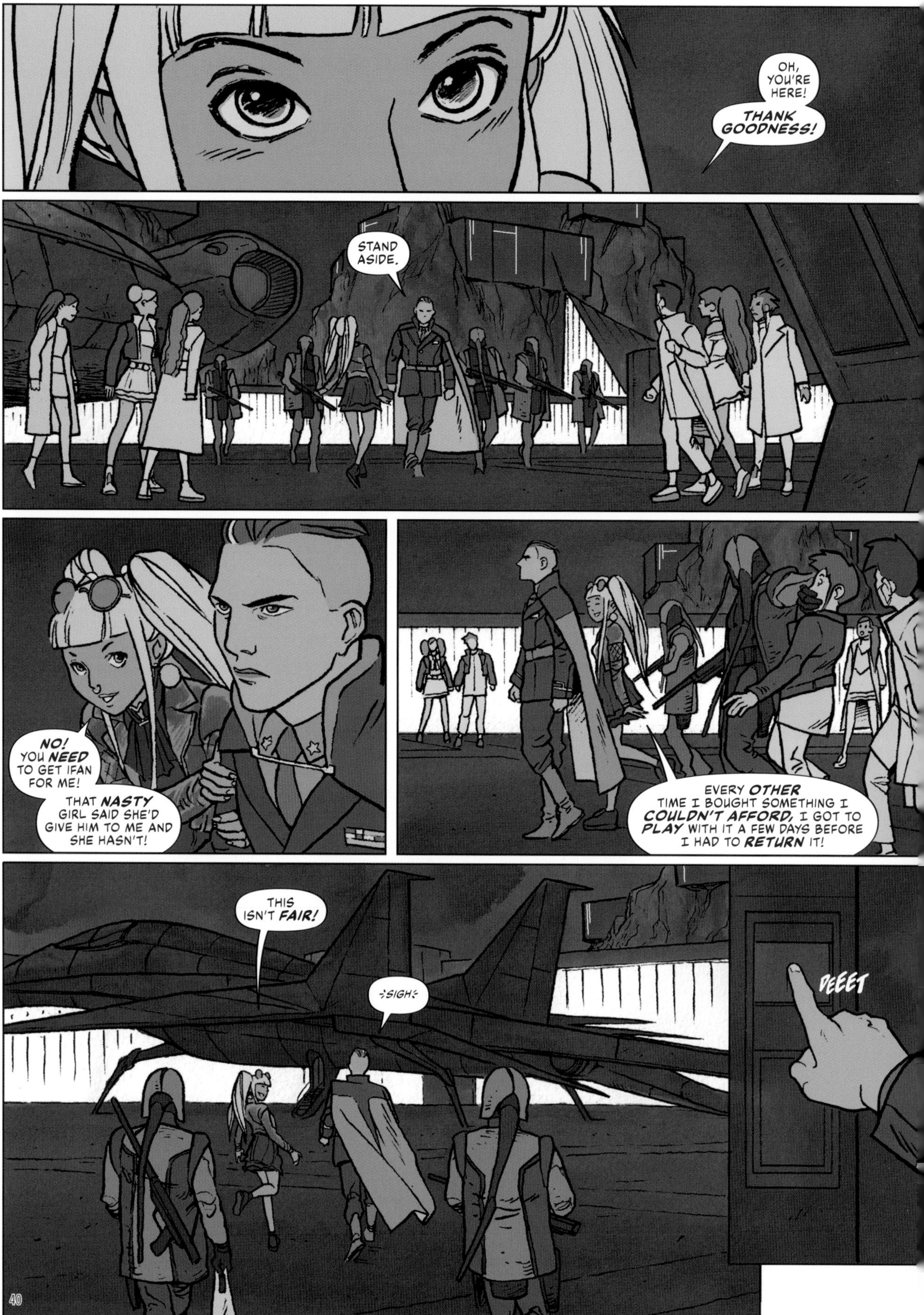
OH, YOU'RE HERE!
THANK GOODNESS!
STAND ASIDE.
NO! YOU NEED TO GET IFAN FOR ME!
THAT NASTY GIRL SAID SHE'D GIVE HIM TO ME AND SHE HASN'T!
EVERY OTHER TIME I BOUGHT SOMETHING I COULDN'T AFFORD, I GOT TO PLAY WITH IT A FEW DAYS BEFORE I HAD TO RETURN IT!
THIS ISN'T FAIR!
SIGH
DEEET

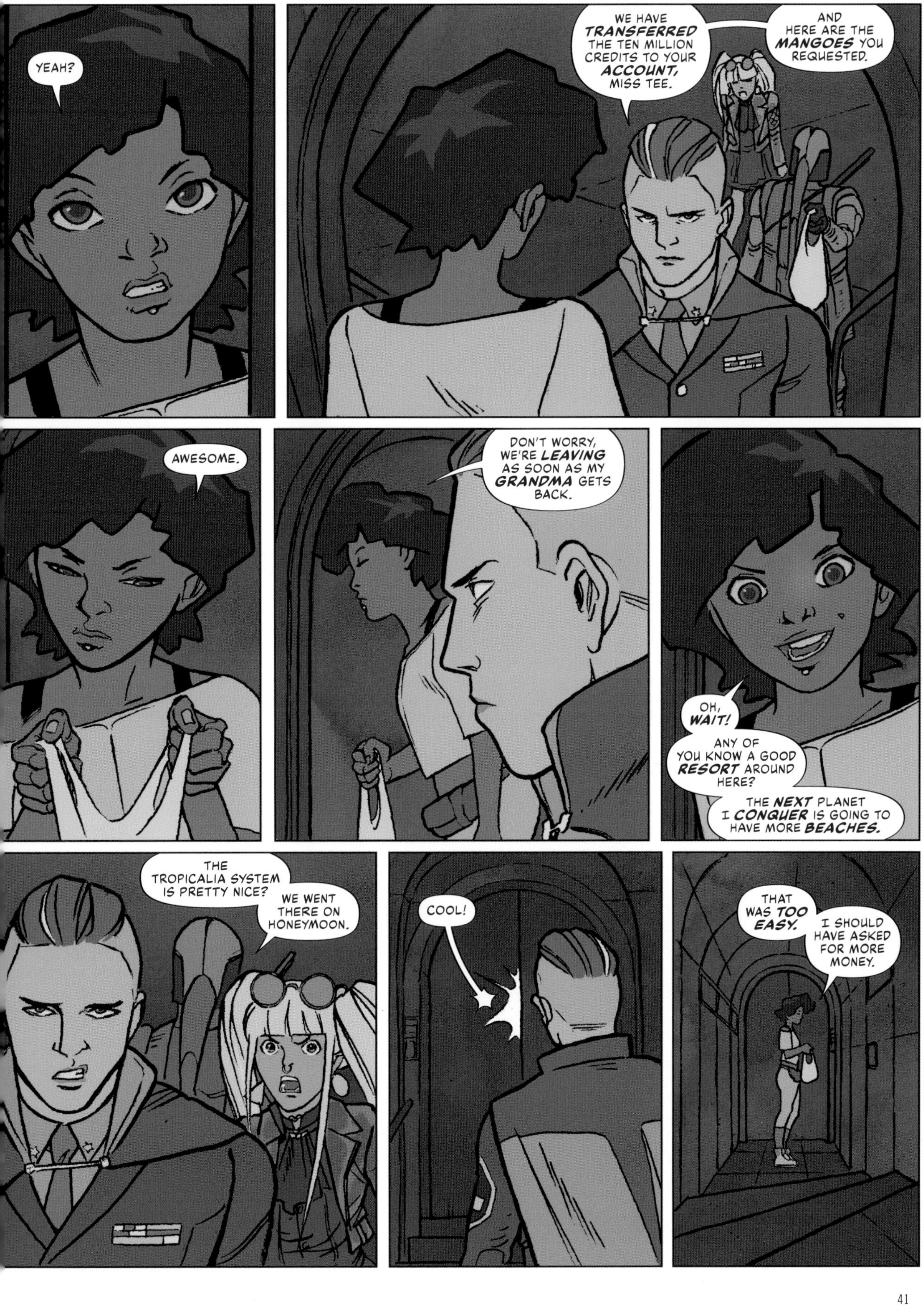
YEAH?
WE HAVE TRANSFERRED THE TEN MILLION CREDITS TO YOUR ACCOUNT, MISS TEE.
AND HERE ARE THE MANGOES YOU REQUESTED.
AWESOME.
DON'T WORRY, WE'RE LEAVING AS SOON AS MY GRANDMA GETS BACK.
OH, WAIT!
ANY OF YOU KNOW A GOOD RESORT AROUND HERE?
THE NEXT PLANET I CONQUER IS GOING TO HAVE MORE BEACHES.
THE TROPICALIA SYSTEM IS PRETTY NICE?
WE WENT THERE ON HONEYMOON.
COOL!
THAT WAS TOO EASY.
I SHOULD HAVE ASKED FOR MORE MONEY.

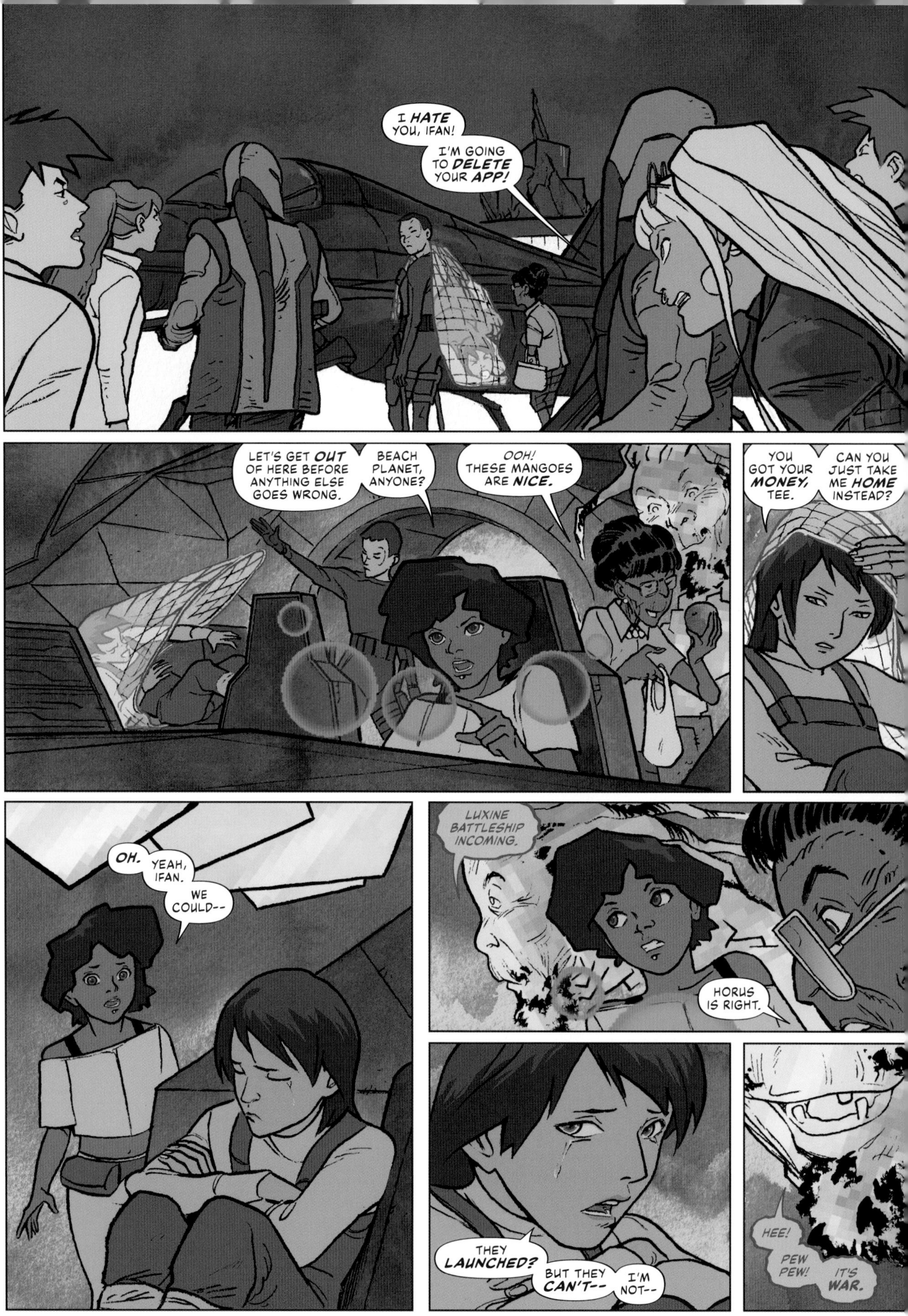

I **HATE** YOU, IFAN!
I'M GOING TO **DELETE** YOUR **APP!**
LET'S GET **OUT** OF HERE BEFORE ANYTHING ELSE GOES WRONG.
BEACH PLANET, ANYONE?
OOH! THESE MANGOES ARE **NICE.**
YOU GOT YOUR **MONEY,** TEE.
CAN YOU JUST TAKE ME **HOME** INSTEAD?
OH.
YEAH, IFAN.
WE COULD--
LUXINE BATTLESHIP INCOMING.
HORUS IS RIGHT.
THEY **LAUNCHED?**
BUT THEY **CAN'T--**
I'M NOT--
HEE!
PEW PEW!
IT'S ***WAR.***

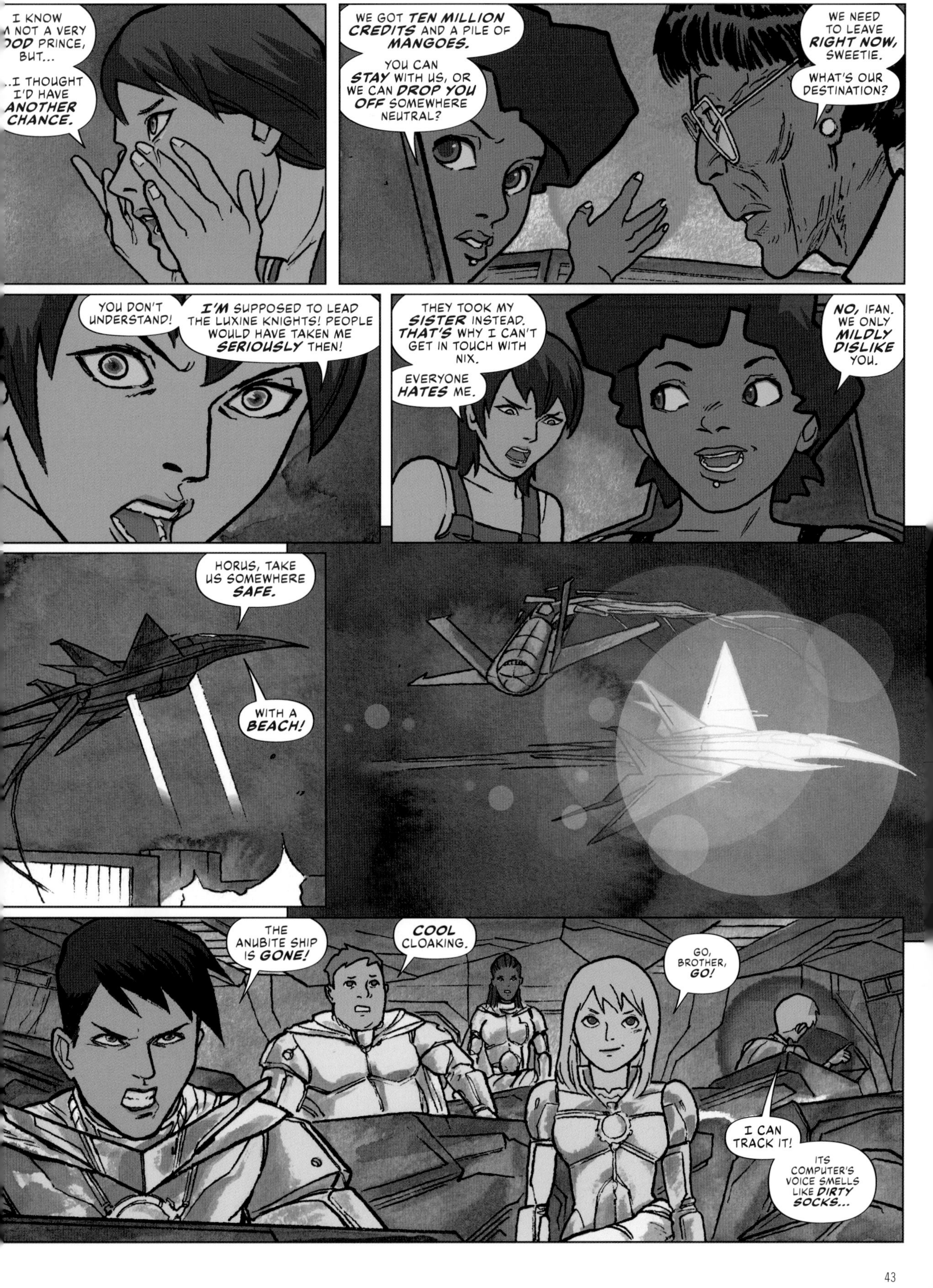
I KNOW
M NOT A VERY
OOD PRINCE,
BUT...
..I THOUGHT I'D HAVE ANOTHER CHANCE.
WE GOT TEN MILLION CREDITS AND A PILE OF MANGOES.
YOU CAN STAY WITH US, OR WE CAN DROP YOU OFF SOMEWHERE NEUTRAL?
WE NEED TO LEAVE RIGHT NOW, SWEETIE.
WHAT'S OUR DESTINATION?
YOU DON'T UNDERSTAND!
I'M SUPPOSED TO LEAD THE LUXINE KNIGHTS! PEOPLE WOULD HAVE TAKEN ME SERIOUSLY THEN!
THEY TOOK MY SISTER INSTEAD. THAT'S WHY I CAN'T GET IN TOUCH WITH NIX.
EVERYONE HATES ME.
NO, IFAN. WE ONLY MILDLY DISLIKE YOU.
HORUS, TAKE US SOMEWHERE SAFE.
WITH A BEACH!
THE ANUBITE SHIP IS GONE!
COOL CLOAKING.
GO, BROTHER, GO!
I CAN TRACK IT!
ITS COMPUTER'S VOICE SMELLS LIKE DIRTY SOCKS...

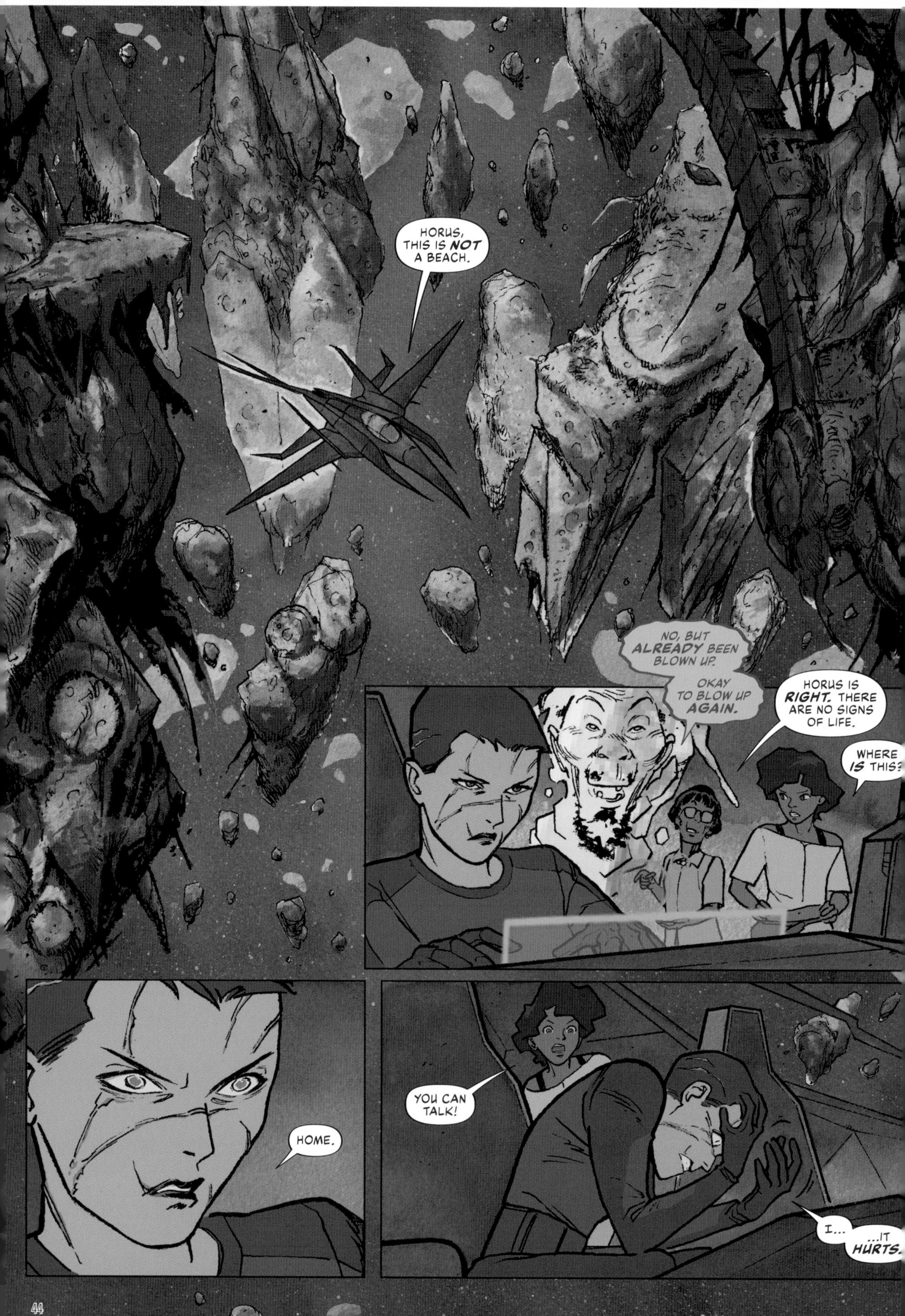
HORUS, THIS IS NOT A BEACH.
NO, BUT ALREADY BEEN BLOWN UP.
OKAY TO BLOW UP AGAIN.
HORUS IS RIGHT. THERE ARE NO SIGNS OF LIFE.
WHERE IS THIS?
HOME.
YOU CAN TALK!
I...
...IT HURTS.

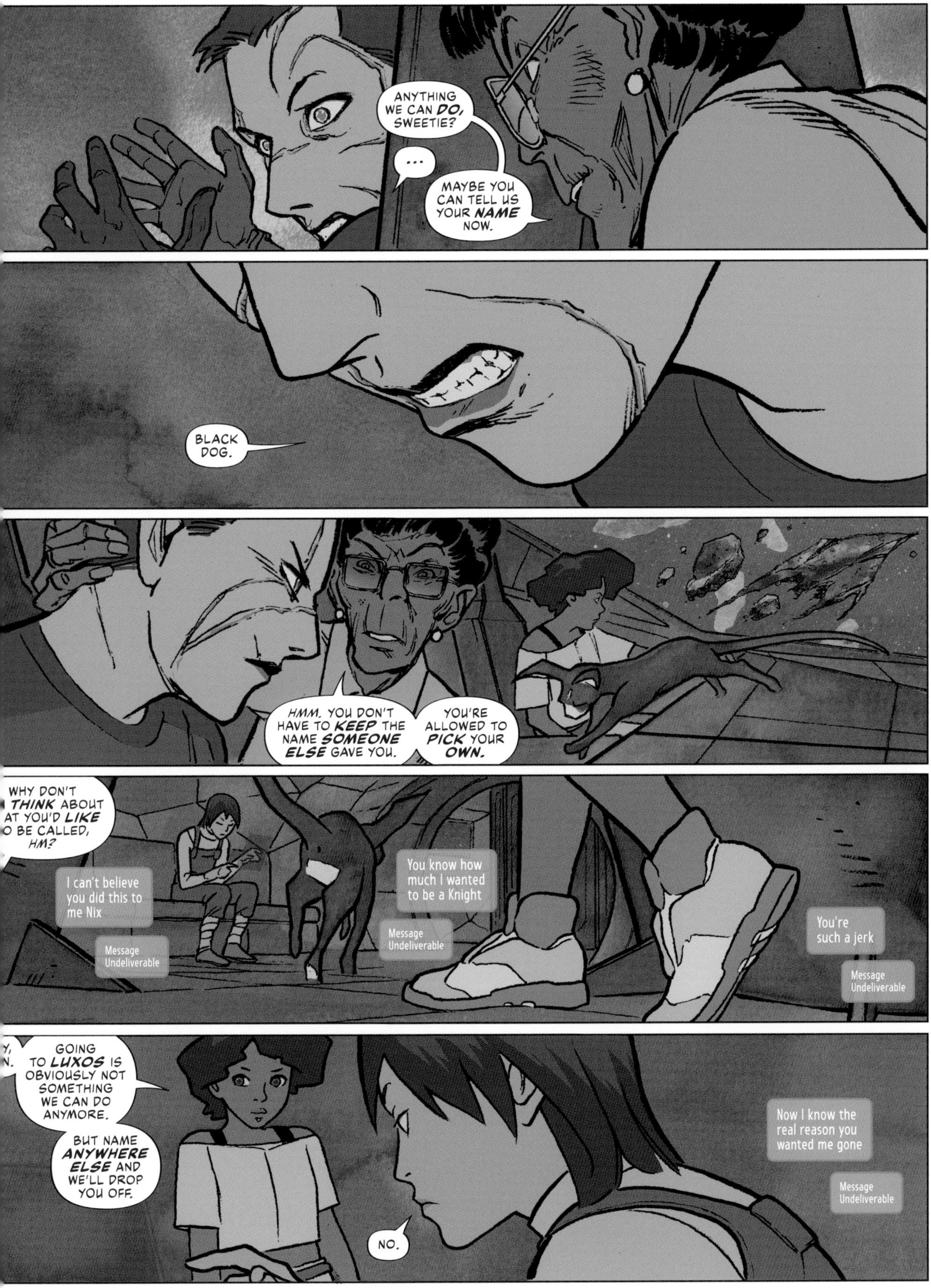
ANYTHING WE CAN DO, SWEETIE?
...
MAYBE YOU CAN TELL US YOUR NAME NOW.
BLACK DOG.
HMM. YOU DON'T HAVE TO KEEP THE NAME SOMEONE ELSE GAVE YOU.
YOU'RE ALLOWED TO PICK YOUR OWN.
WHY DON'T THINK ABOUT AT YOU'D LIKE O BE CALLED, HM?
I can't believe you did this to me Nix
Message Undeliverable
You know how much I wanted to be a Knight
Message Undeliverable
You're such a jerk
Message Undeliverable
GOING TO LUXOS IS OBVIOUSLY NOT SOMETHING WE CAN DO ANYMORE.
BUT NAME ANYWHERE ELSE AND WE'LL DROP YOU OFF.
Now I know the real reason you wanted me gone
Message Undeliverable
NO.

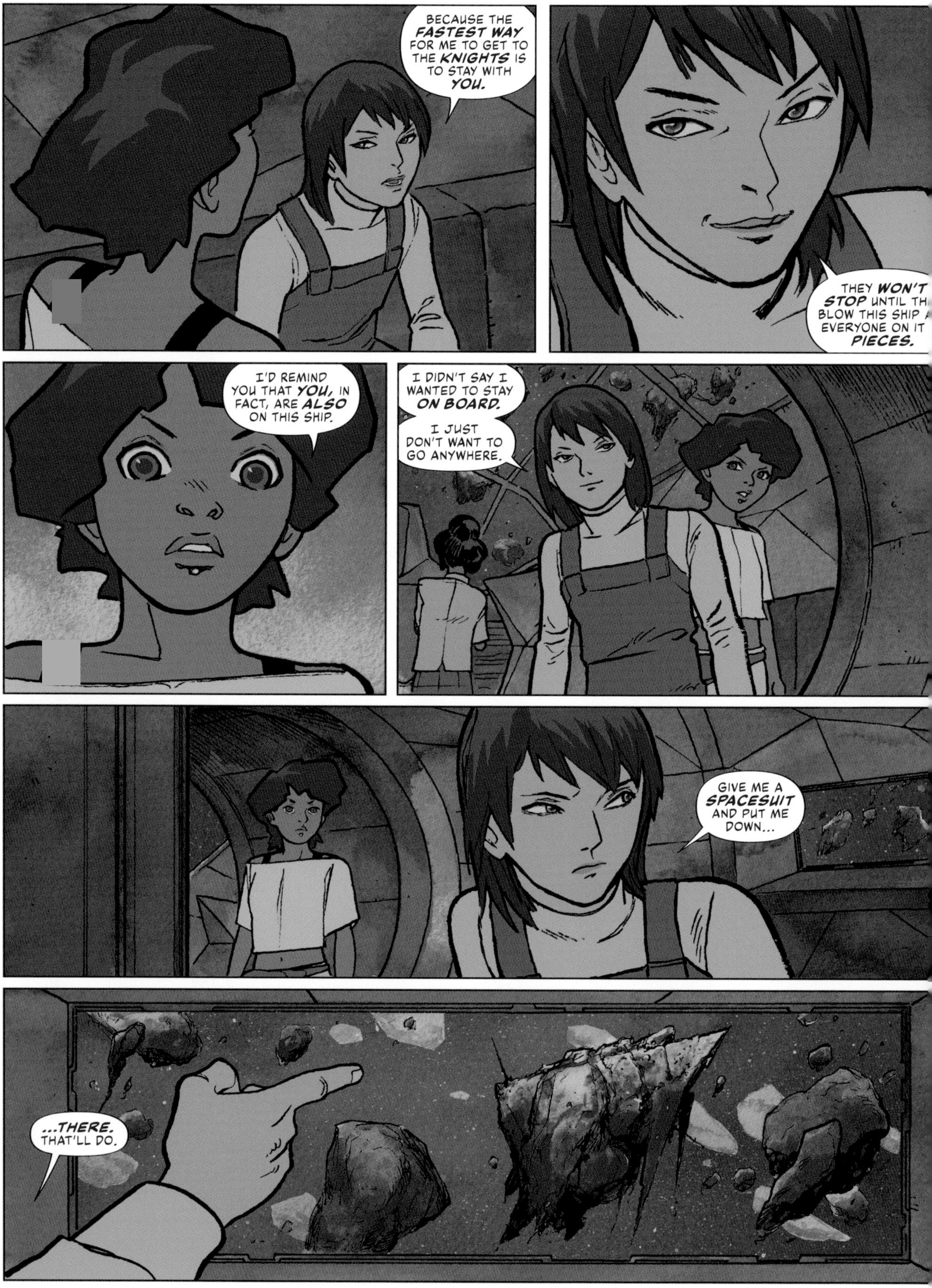
BECAUSE THE FASTEST WAY FOR ME TO GET TO THE KNIGHTS IS TO STAY WITH YOU.
THEY WON'T STOP UNTIL BLOW THIS SHIP EVERYONE ON IT PIECES.
I'D REMIND YOU THAT YOU, IN FACT, ARE ALSO ON THIS SHIP.
I DIDN'T SAY I WANTED TO STAY ON BOARD.
I JUST DON'T WANT TO GO ANYWHERE.
GIVE ME A SPACESUIT AND PUT ME DOWN...
...THERE. THAT'LL DO.

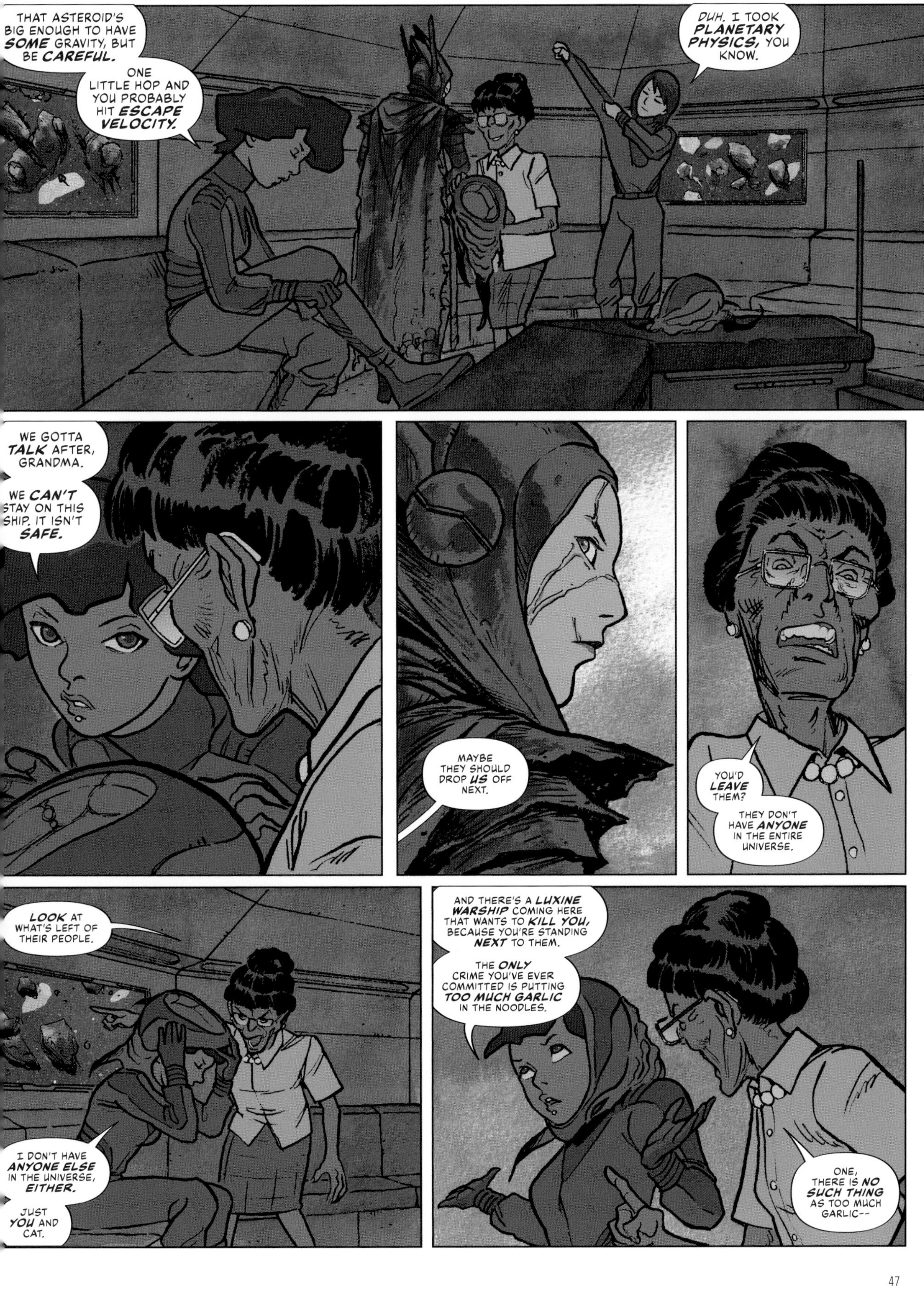

THAT ASTEROID'S BIG ENOUGH TO HAVE SOME GRAVITY, BUT BE CAREFUL.
ONE LITTLE HOP AND YOU PROBABLY HIT ESCAPE VELOCITY.
DUH. I TOOK PLANETARY PHYSICS, YOU KNOW.
WE GOTTA TALK AFTER, GRANDMA.
WE CAN'T STAY ON THIS SHIP. IT ISN'T SAFE.
MAYBE THEY SHOULD DROP US OFF NEXT.
YOU'D LEAVE THEM?
THEY DON'T HAVE ANYONE IN THE ENTIRE UNIVERSE.
LOOK AT WHAT'S LEFT OF THEIR PEOPLE.
I DON'T HAVE ANYONE ELSE IN THE UNIVERSE, EITHER.
JUST YOU AND CAT.
AND THERE'S A LUXINE WARSHIP COMING HERE THAT WANTS TO KILL YOU, BECAUSE YOU'RE STANDING NEXT TO THEM.
THE ONLY CRIME YOU'VE EVER COMMITTED IS PUTTING TOO MUCH GARLIC IN THE NOODLES.
ONE, THERE IS NO SUCH THING AS TOO MUCH GARLIC--

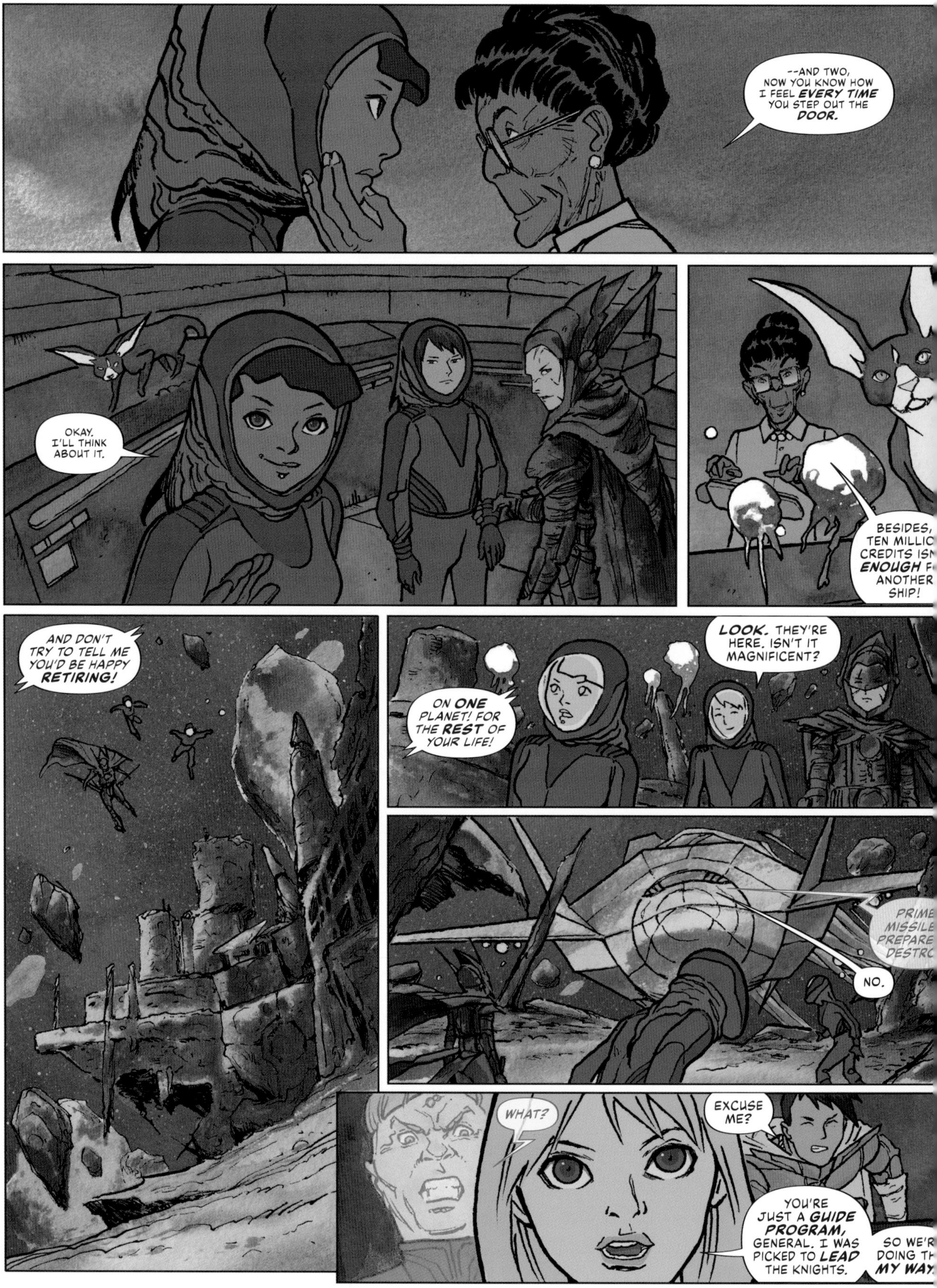

--AND TWO, NOW YOU KNOW HOW I FEEL EVERY TIME YOU STEP OUT THE DOOR.
OKAY. I'LL THINK ABOUT IT.
BESIDES, TEN MILLIO CREDITS ISN ENOUGH F ANOTHER SHIP!
AND DON'T TRY TO TELL ME YOU'D BE HAPPY RETIRING!
ON ONE PLANET! FOR THE REST OF YOUR LIFE!
LOOK. THEY'RE HERE. ISN'T IT MAGNIFICENT?
PRIME MISSILE PREPARE DESTRO
NO.
WHAT?
EXCUSE ME?
YOU'RE JUST A GUIDE PROGRAM, GENERAL. I WAS PICKED TO LEAD THE KNIGHTS.
SO WE'R DOING TH MY WAY

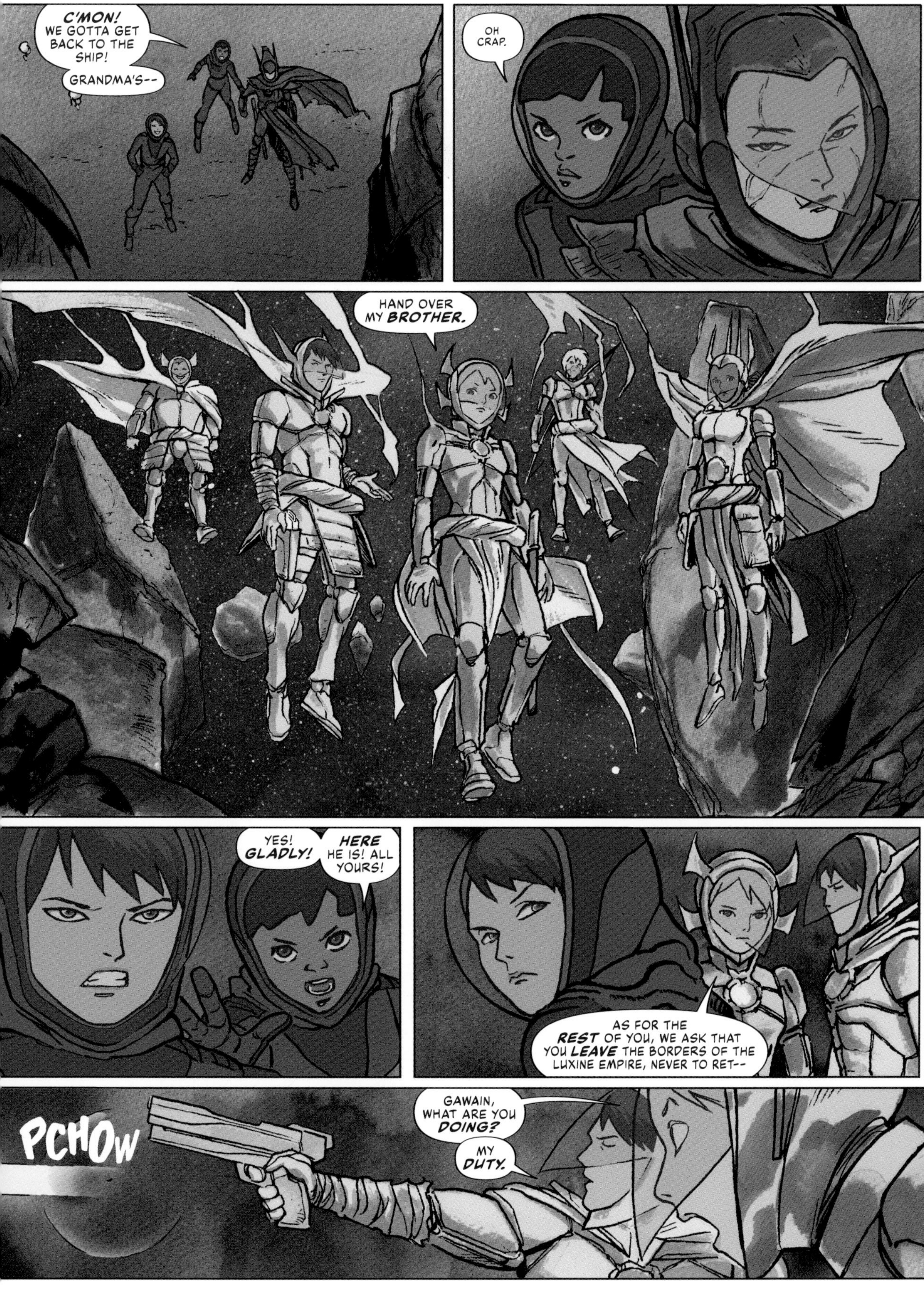
C'MON! WE GOTTA GET BACK TO THE SHIP!
GRANDMA'S--
OH CRAP.
HAND OVER MY BROTHER.
YES! GLADLY!
HERE HE IS! ALL YOURS!
AS FOR THE REST OF YOU, WE ASK THAT YOU LEAVE THE BORDERS OF THE LUXINE EMPIRE, NEVER TO RET--
PCHOW
GAWAIN, WHAT ARE YOU DOING?
MY DUTY.

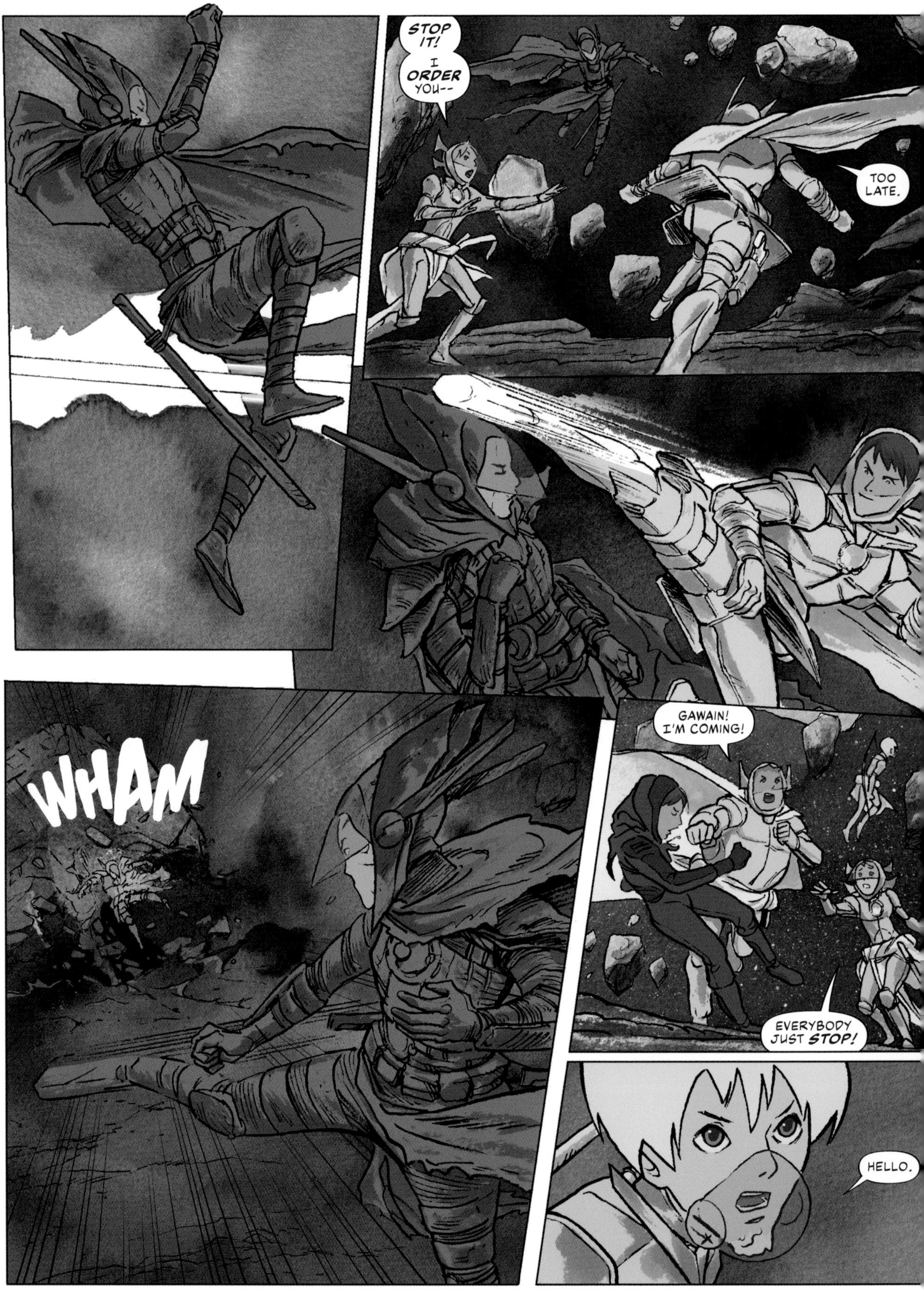
STOP IT! I ORDER YOU--
TOO LATE.
WHAM
GAWAIN! I'M COMING!
EVERYBODY JUST STOP!
HELLO.

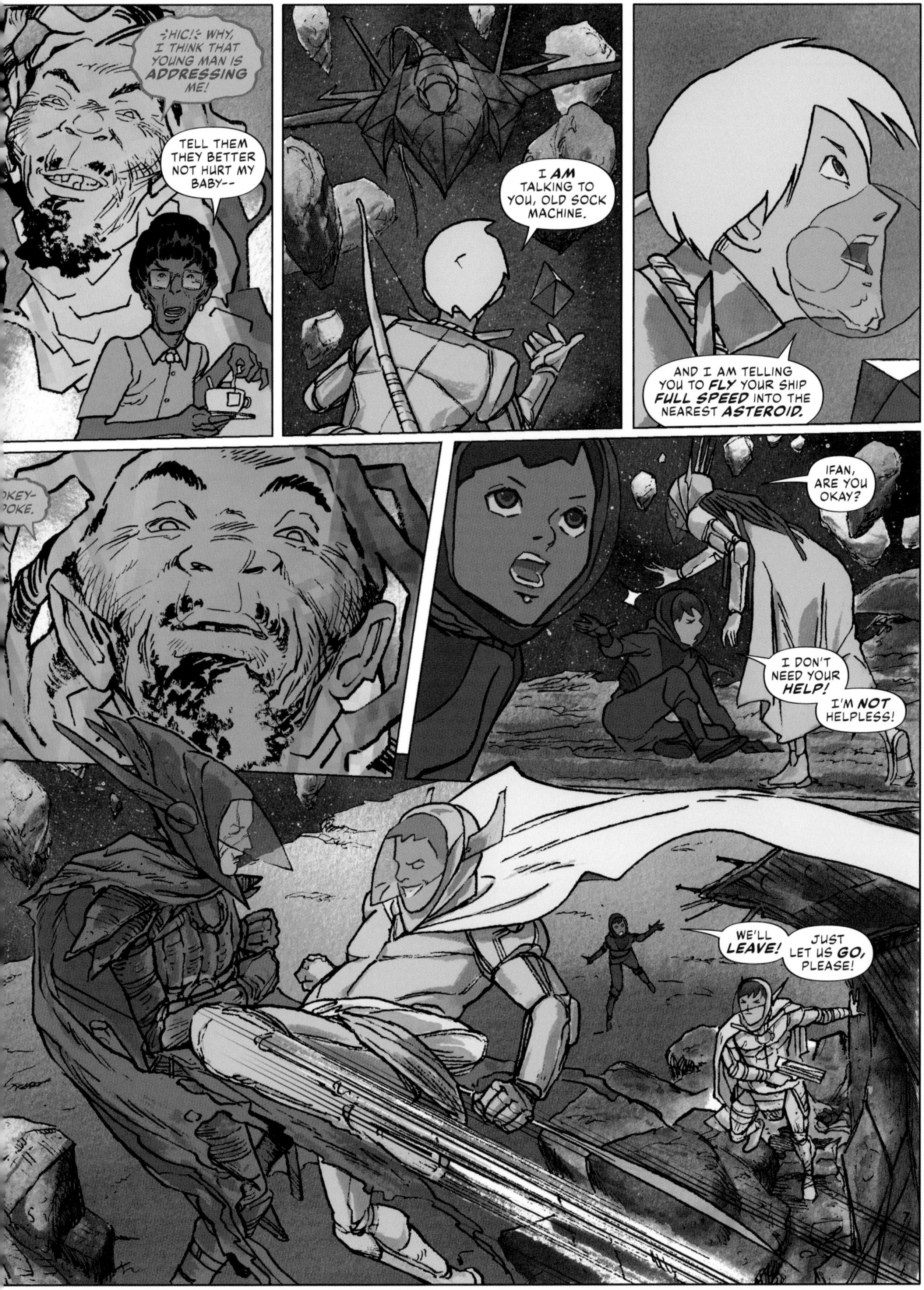

HIC! WHY, I THINK THAT YOUNG MAN IS ADDRESSING ME!
TELL THEM THEY BETTER NOT HURT MY BABY--
I AM TALKING TO YOU, OLD SOCK MACHINE.
AND I AM TELLING YOU TO FLY YOUR SHIP FULL SPEED INTO THE NEAREST ASTEROID.
OKEY-OKE.
IFAN, ARE YOU OKAY?
I DON'T NEED YOUR HELP!
I'M NOT HELPLESS!
WE'LL LEAVE!
JUST LET US GO, PLEASE!

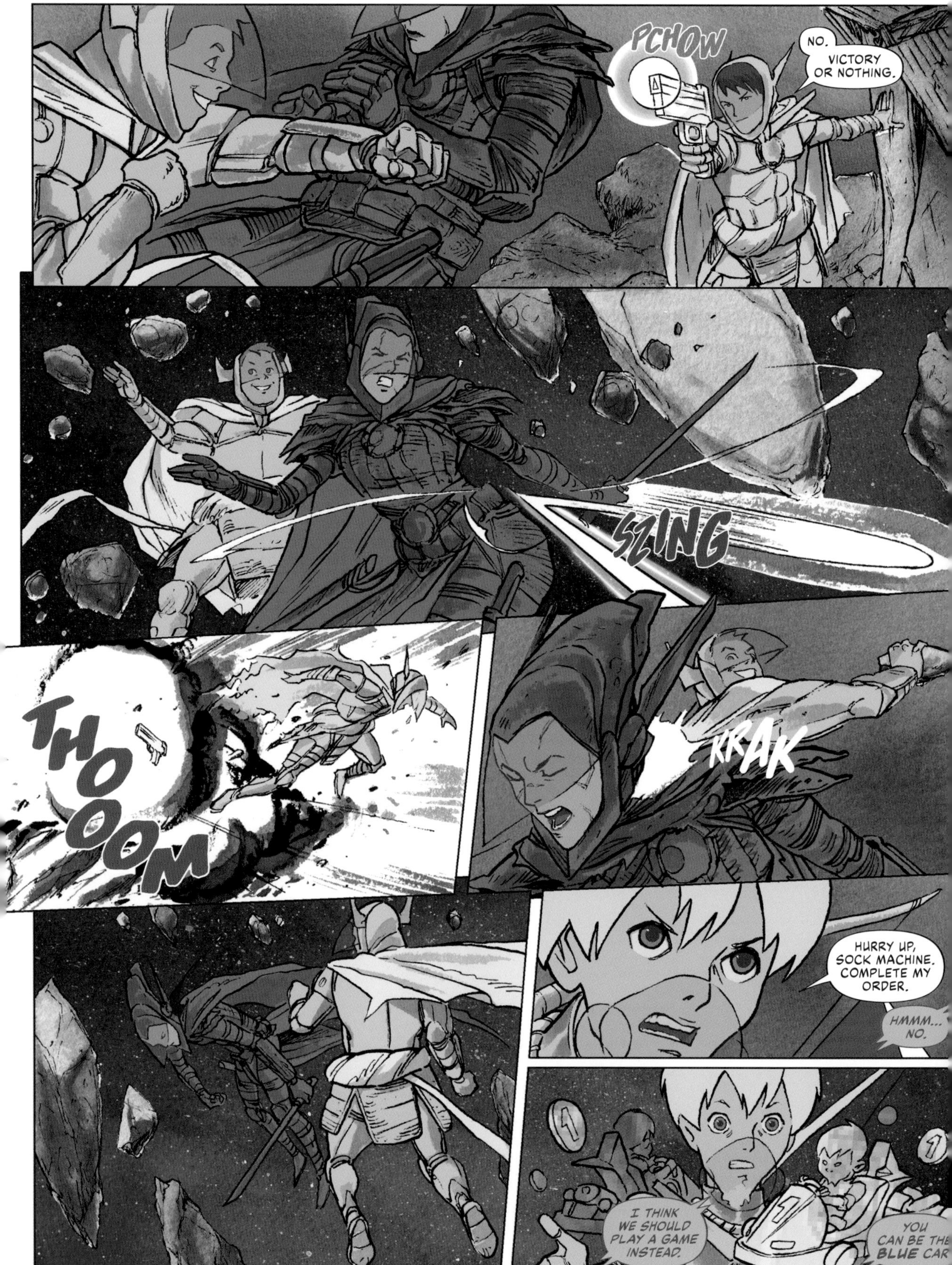
PCHOW
NO.
VICTORY OR NOTHING.
SZING
THOOOM
KRAK
HURRY UP, SOCK MACHINE. COMPLETE MY ORDER.
HMMM... NO.
I THINK WE SHOULD PLAY A GAME INSTEAD.
YOU CAN BE THE BLUE CAR

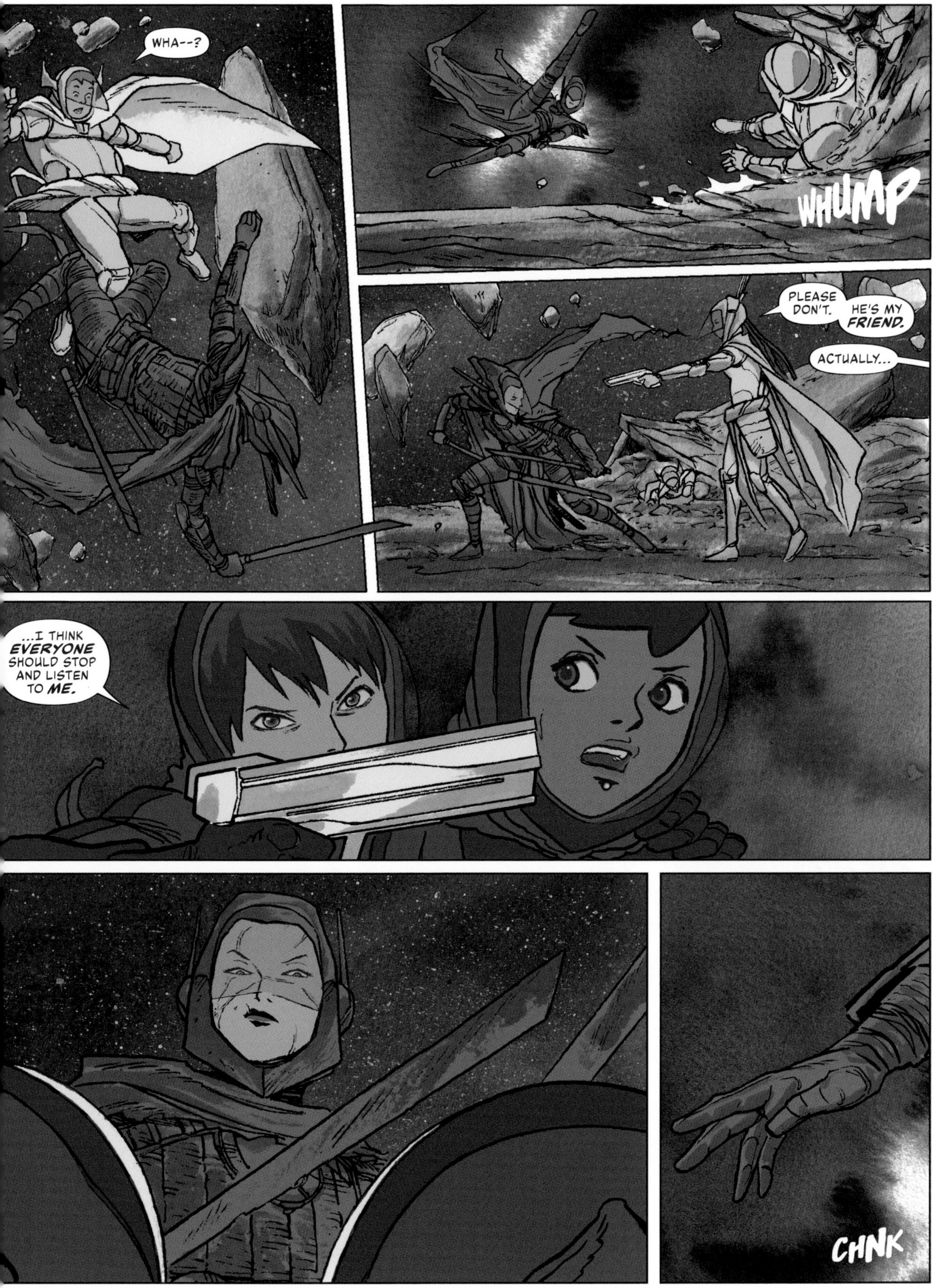
WHA--?
WHUMP
PLEASE DON'T.
HE'S MY FRIEND.
ACTUALLY...
...I THINK EVERYONE SHOULD STOP AND LISTEN TO ME.
CHNK

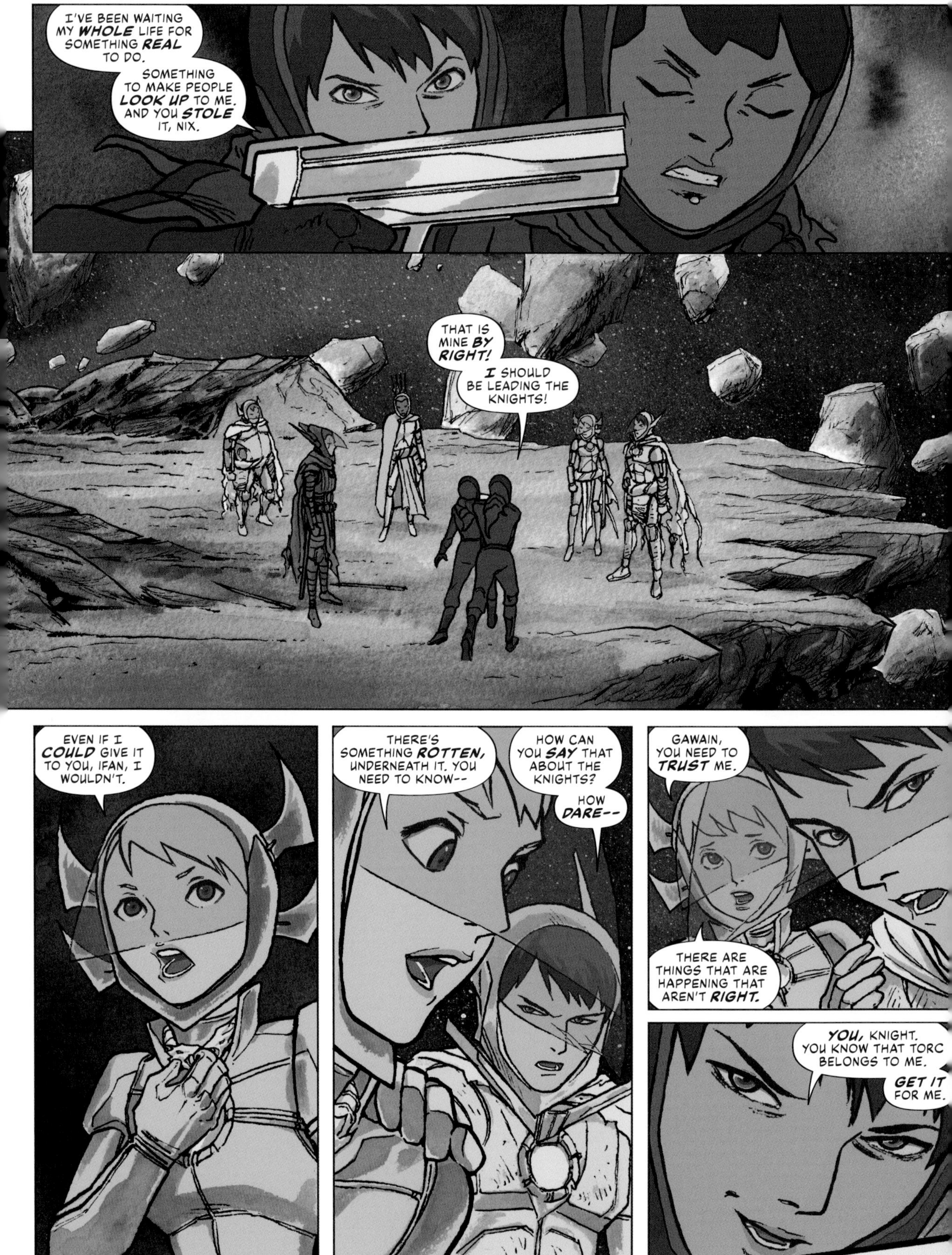
I'VE BEEN WAITING MY WHOLE LIFE FOR SOMETHING REAL TO DO.
SOMETHING TO MAKE PEOPLE LOOK UP TO ME. AND YOU STOLE IT, NIX.
THAT IS MINE BY RIGHT!
I SHOULD BE LEADING THE KNIGHTS!
EVEN IF I COULD GIVE IT TO YOU, IFAN, I WOULDN'T.
THERE'S SOMETHING ROTTEN, UNDERNEATH IT. YOU NEED TO KNOW--
HOW CAN YOU SAY THAT ABOUT THE KNIGHTS?
HOW DARE--
GAWAIN, YOU NEED TO TRUST ME.
THERE ARE THINGS THAT ARE HAPPENING THAT AREN'T RIGHT.
YOU, KNIGHT. YOU KNOW THAT TORC BELONGS TO ME.
GET IT FOR ME.

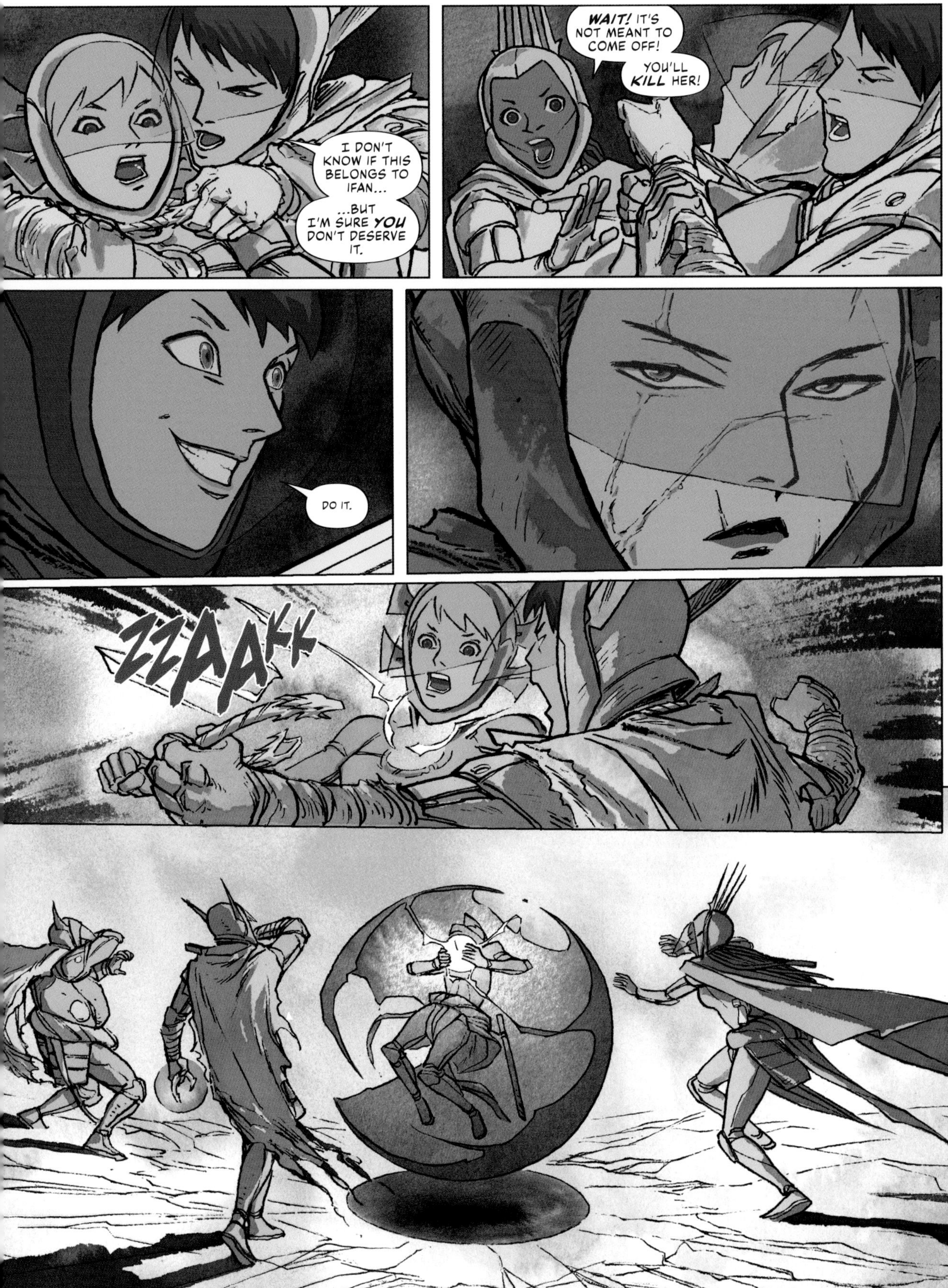
I DON'T KNOW IF THIS BELONGS TO IFAN...
...BUT I'M SURE ***YOU*** DON'T DESERVE IT.
WAIT! IT'S NOT MEANT TO COME OFF!
YOU'LL ***KILL*** HER!
DO IT.
ZZAPAKK

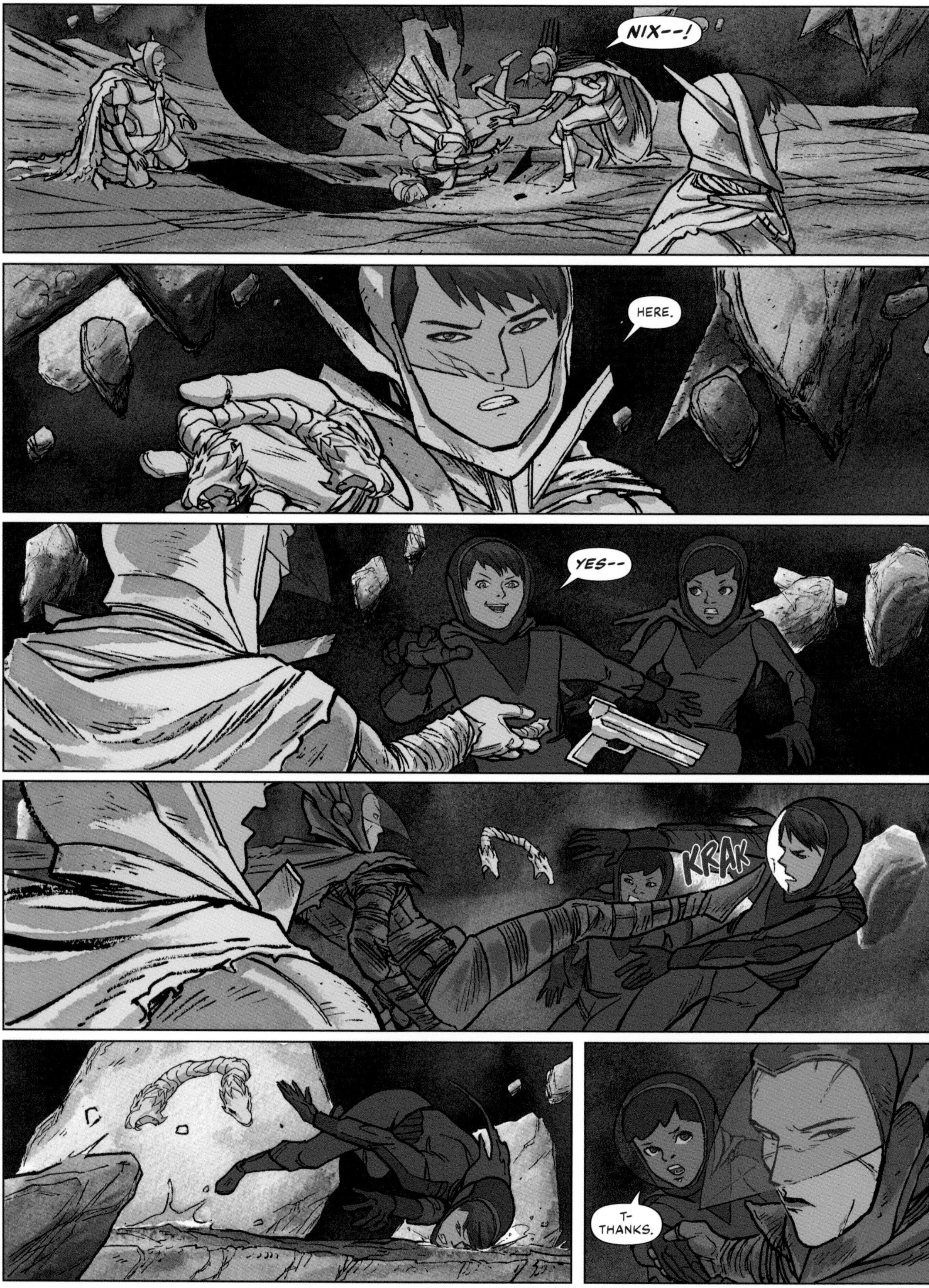
NIX--!
HERE.
YES--
KRAK
T- THANKS.

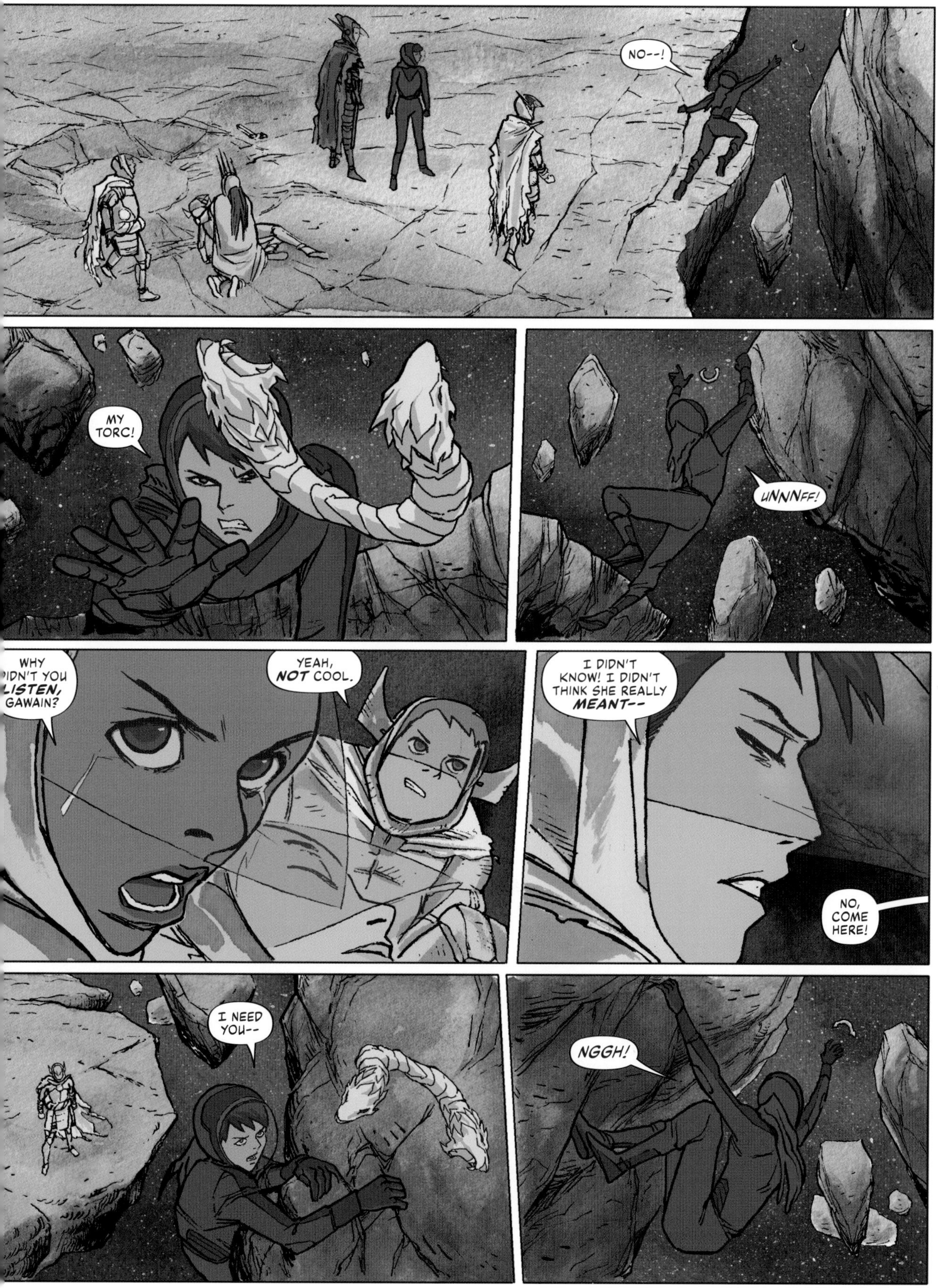
NO--!
MY TORC!
UNNNFF!
WHY DIDN'T YOU LISTEN, GAWAIN?
YEAH, NOT COOL.
I DIDN'T KNOW! I DIDN'T THINK SHE REALLY MEANT--
NO, COME HERE!
I NEED YOU--
NGGH!

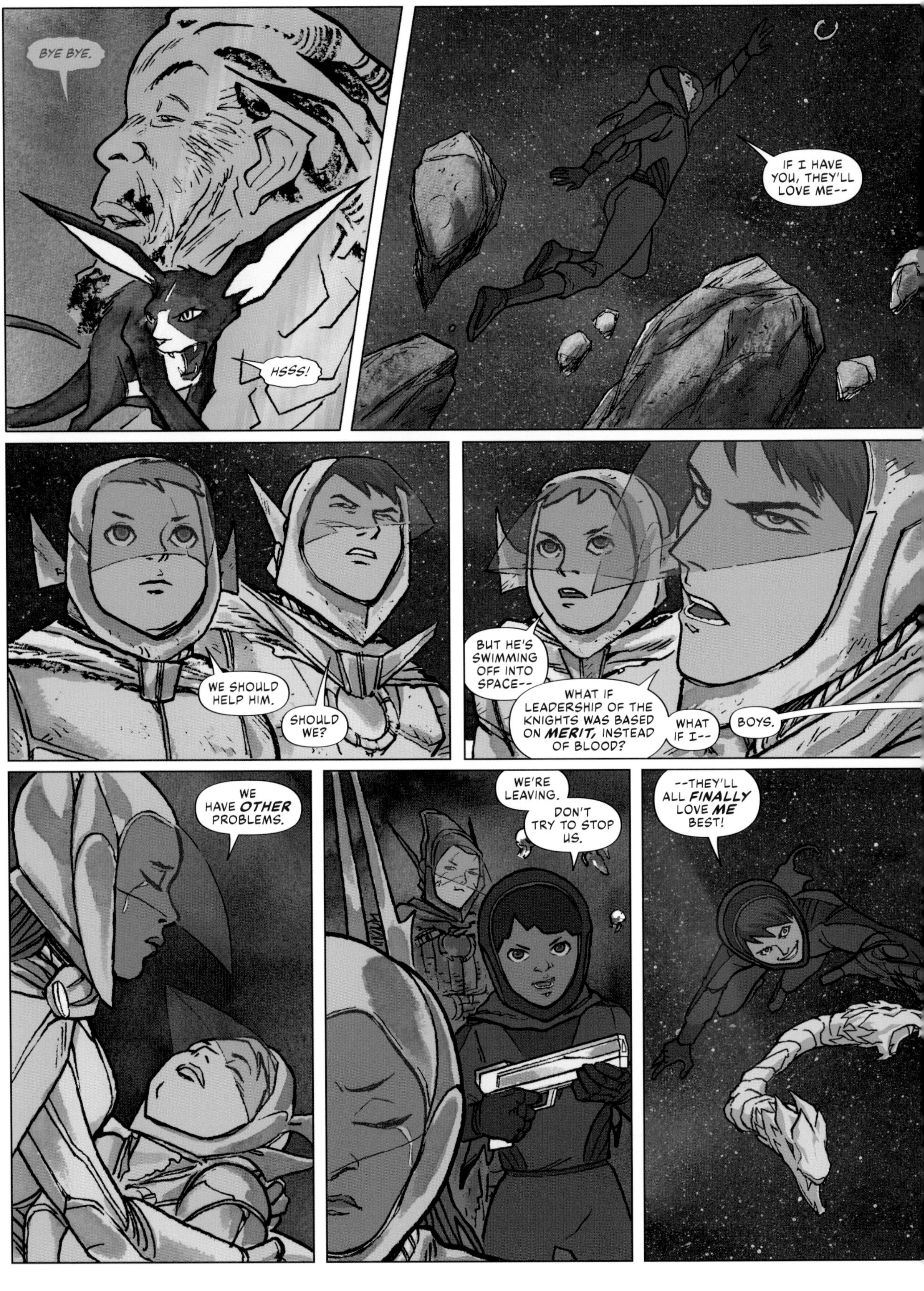
BYE BYE.
HSSS!
IF I HAVE YOU, THEY'LL LOVE ME--
WE SHOULD HELP HIM.
SHOULD WE?
BUT HE'S SWIMMING OFF INTO SPACE--
WHAT IF LEADERSHIP OF THE KNIGHTS WAS BASED ON MERIT, INSTEAD OF BLOOD?
WHAT IF I--
BOYS.
WE HAVE OTHER PROBLEMS.
WE'RE LEAVING.
DON'T TRY TO STOP US.
--THEY'LL ALL FINALLY LOVE ME BEST!

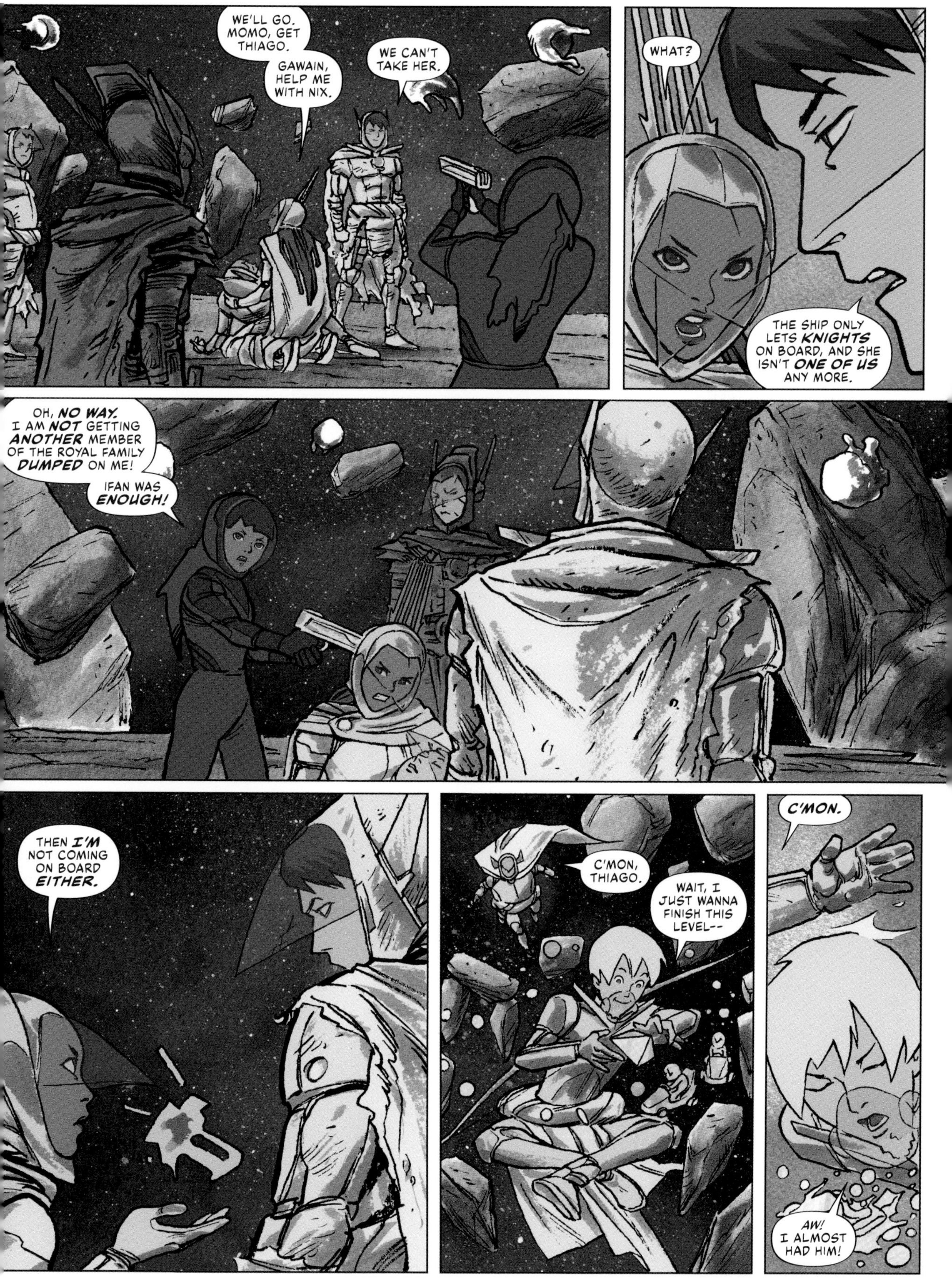
WE'LL GO. MOMO, GET THIAGO.
GAWAIN, HELP ME WITH NIX.
WE CAN'T TAKE HER.
WHAT?
THE SHIP ONLY LETS KNIGHTS ON BOARD, AND SHE ISN'T ONE OF US ANY MORE.
OH, NO WAY. I AM NOT GETTING ANOTHER MEMBER OF THE ROYAL FAMILY DUMPED ON ME!
IFAN WAS ENOUGH!
THEN I'M NOT COMING ON BOARD EITHER.
C'MON, THIAGO.
WAIT, I JUST WANNA FINISH THIS LEVEL--
C'MON.
AW! I ALMOST HAD HIM!

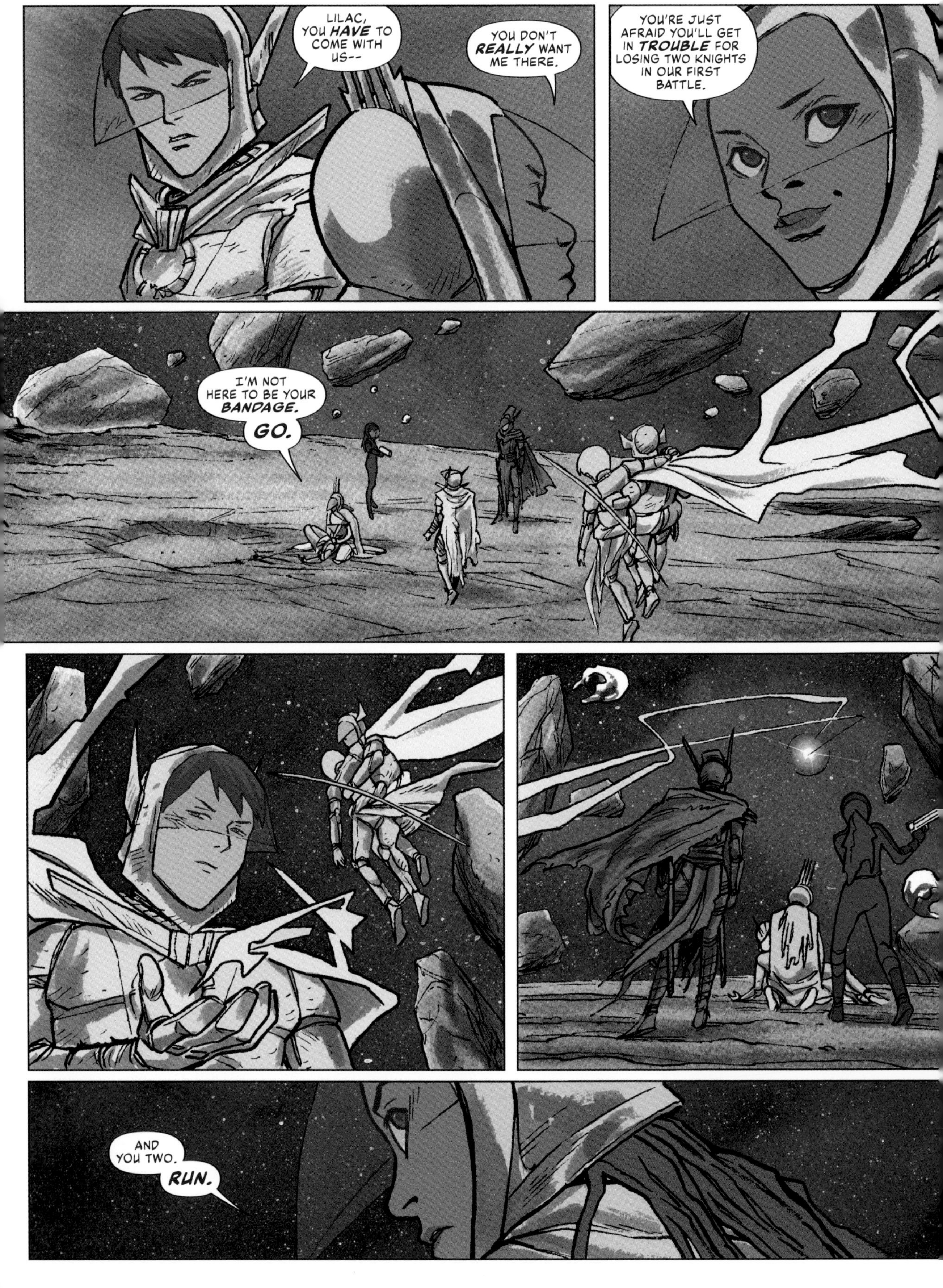
LILAC, YOU HAVE TO COME WITH US--
YOU DON'T REALLY WANT ME THERE.
YOU'RE JUST AFRAID YOU'LL GET IN TROUBLE FOR LOSING TWO KNIGHTS IN OUR FIRST BATTLE.
I'M NOT HERE TO BE YOUR BANDAGE.
GO.
AND YOU TWO.
RUN.

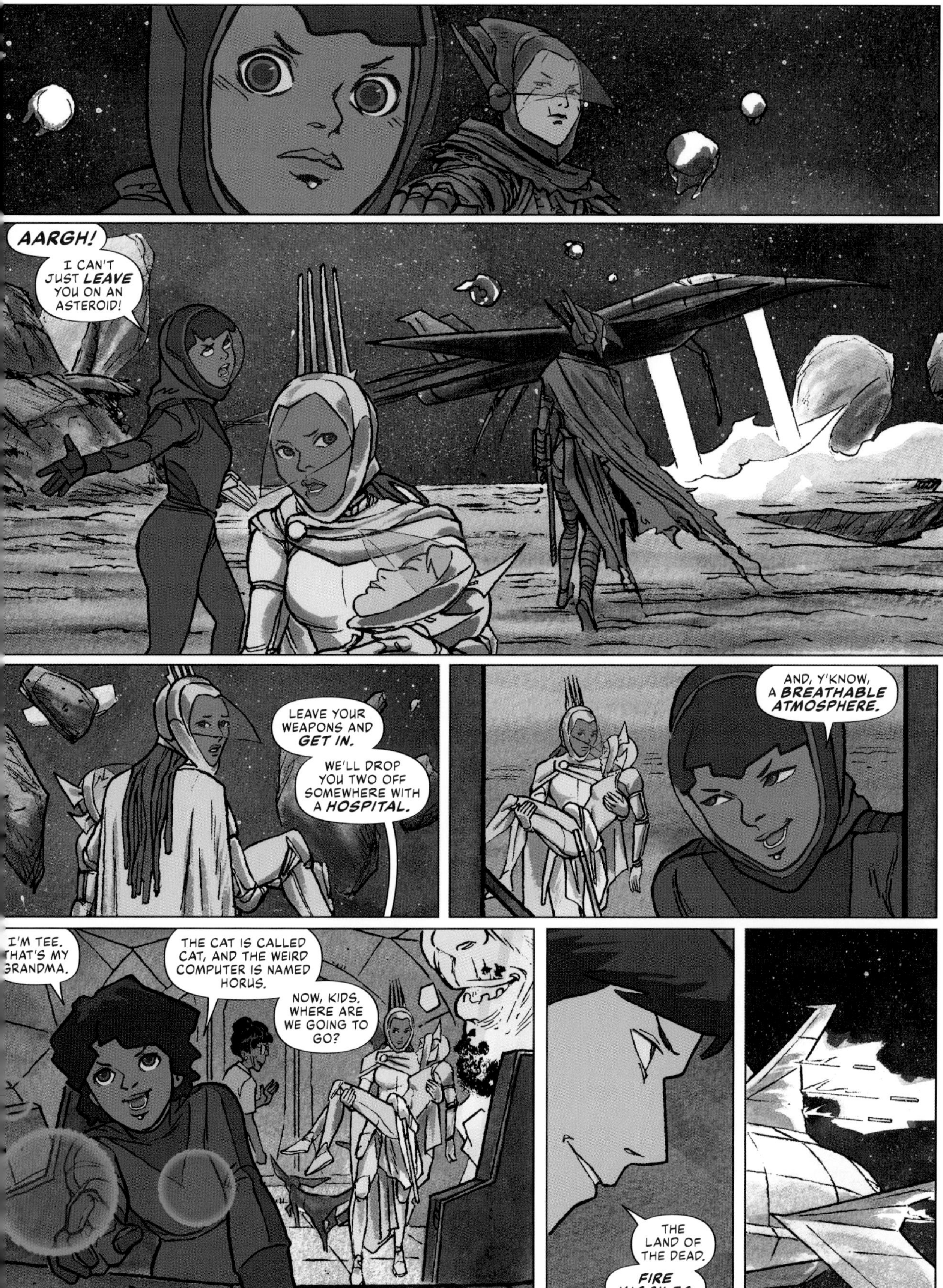
AARGH!
I CAN'T JUST LEAVE YOU ON AN ASTEROID!
LEAVE YOUR WEAPONS AND GET IN.
WE'LL DROP YOU TWO OFF SOMEWHERE WITH A HOSPITAL.
AND, Y'KNOW, A BREATHABLE ATMOSPHERE.
I'M TEE. THAT'S MY GRANDMA.
THE CAT IS CALLED CAT, AND THE WEIRD COMPUTER IS NAMED HORUS.
NOW, KIDS. WHERE ARE WE GOING TO GO?
THE LAND OF THE DEAD.
FIRE MISSILES.

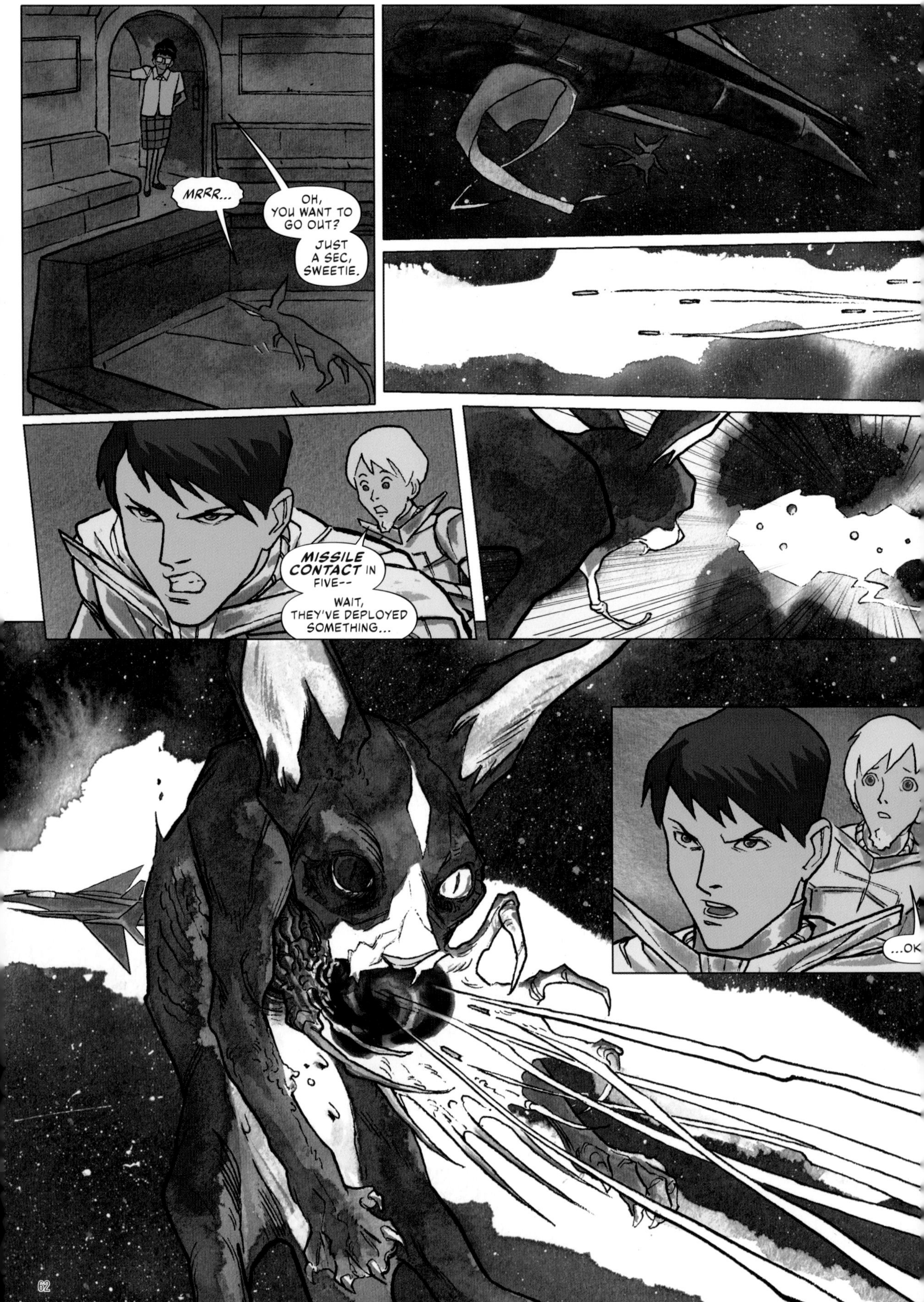
MRRR...
OH, YOU WANT TO GO OUT?
JUST A SEC, SWEETIE.
MISSILE CONTACT IN FIVE--
WAIT, THEY'VE DEPLOYED SOMETHING...
...OK

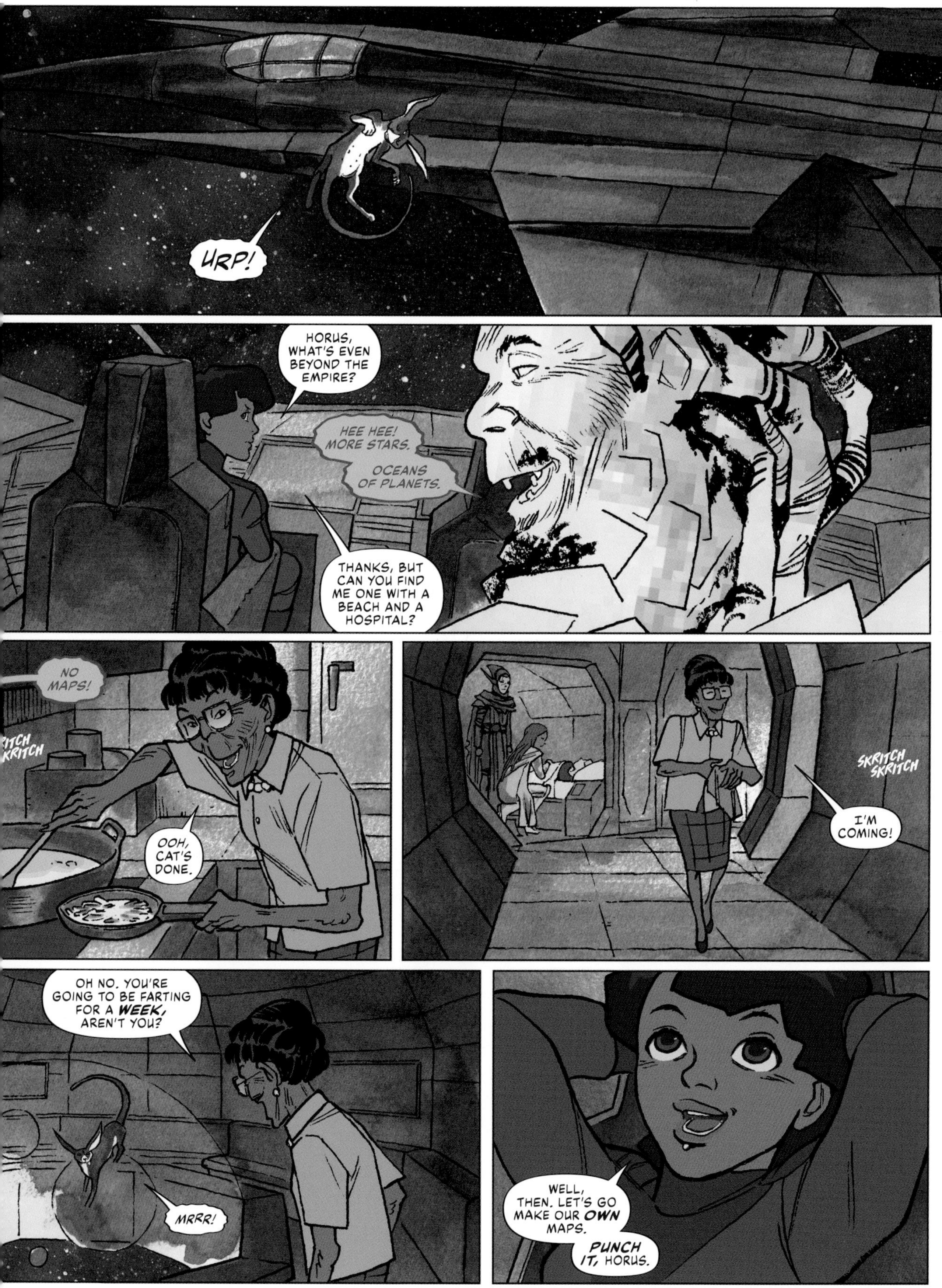
URP!
HORUS, WHAT'S EVEN BEYOND THE EMPIRE?
HEE HEE! MORE STARS.
OCEANS OF PLANETS.
THANKS, BUT CAN YOU FIND ME ONE WITH A BEACH AND A HOSPITAL?
NO MAPS!
SKRITCH SKRITCH
OOH, CAT'S DONE.
SKRITCH SKRITCH
I'M COMING!
OH NO. YOU'RE GOING TO BE FARTING FOR A WEEK, AREN'T YOU?
MRRR!
WELL, THEN. LET'S GO MAKE OUR OWN MAPS.
PUNCH IT, HORUS.

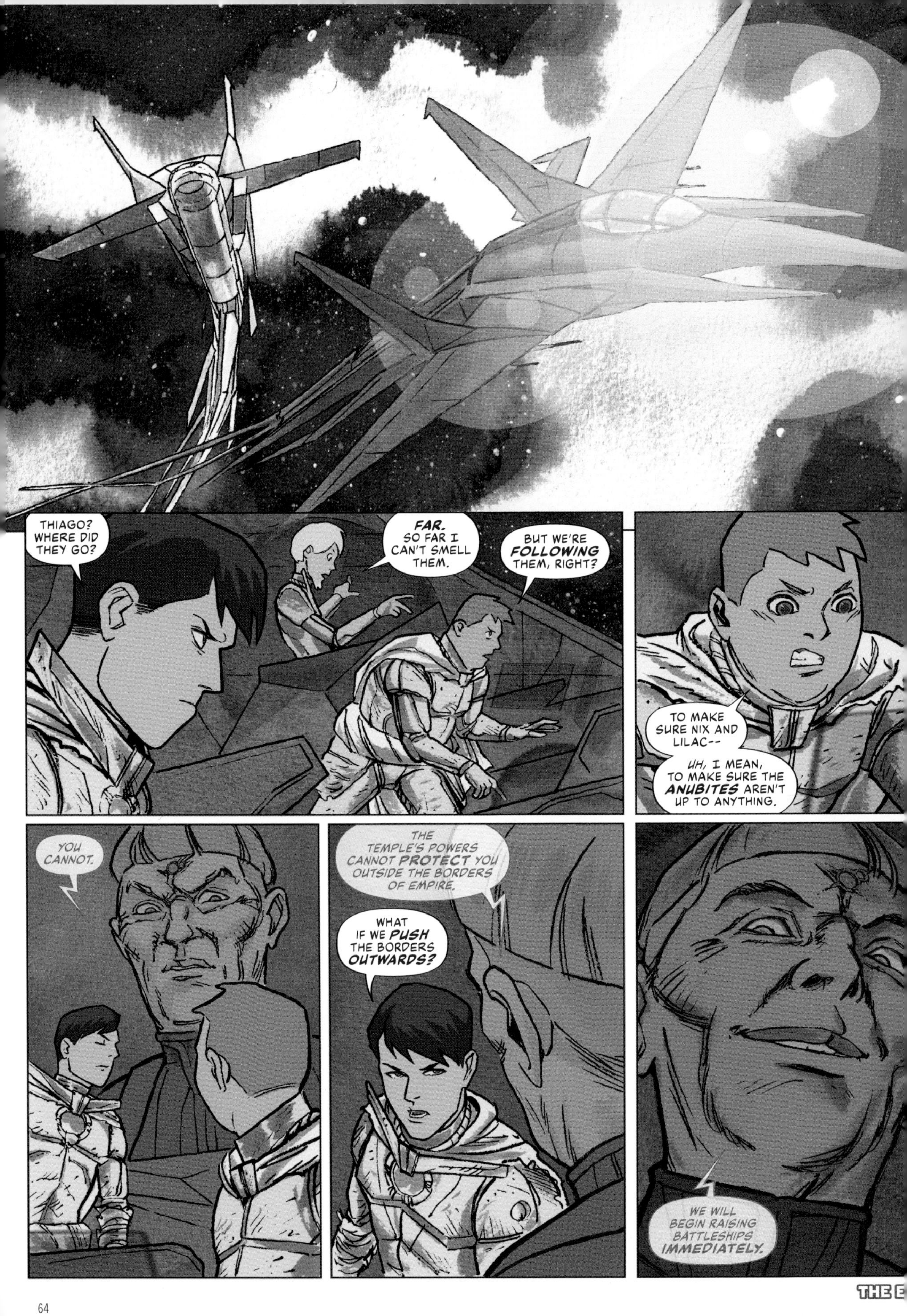
THIAGO? WHERE DID THEY GO?
FAR. SO FAR I CAN'T SMELL THEM.
BUT WE'RE FOLLOWING THEM, RIGHT?
TO MAKE SURE NIX AND LILAC--
UH, I MEAN, TO MAKE SURE THE ANUBITES AREN'T UP TO ANYTHING.
YOU CANNOT.
THE TEMPLE'S POWERS CANNOT PROTECT YOU OUTSIDE THE BORDERS OF EMPIRE.
WHAT IF WE PUSH THE BORDERS OUTWARDS?
WE WILL BEGIN RAISING BATTLESHIPS IMMEDIATELY.
THE E